THE HISTORY OF THE PANZERWAFFE
VOLUME 1: 1939–42

THE HISTORY OF THE PANZERWAFFE

VOLUME 1: 1939–42

Thomas Anderson

First published in Great Britain in 2015 by Osprey Publishing,
PO Box 883, Oxford, OX1 9PL, UK
PO Box 3985, New York, NY 10185-3985, USA
E-mail: info@ospreypublishing.com

Osprey Publishing is part of Bloomsbury Publishing Plc.
© 2015 Osprey Publishing

Every attempt has been made by the Publisher to secure the
appropriate permissions for material reproduced in this book. If there
has been any oversight we will be happy to rectify the situation and
written submission should be made to the Publishers. A CIP catalogue
record for this book is available from the British Library

Print ISBN: 978 1 4728 0812 7
e-book ISBN: 978 1 4728 1360 2
epub ISBN: 978 1 4728 1361 9

Conceived and edited by Jasper Spencer-Smith.
Design and artwork: Nigel Pell.
Index by Shaun Barrington.
Produced by Editworks Limited,
Bournemouth BH1 4RT, England.
Printed in China through Worldprint Ltd.

11 12 13 14 15   10 9 8 7 6 5 4 3 2 1

Osprey Publishing is supporting the Woodland Trust, the UK's leading
woodland conservation charity, by funding the dedication of trees.

www.ospreypublishing.com

CONTENTS

INTRODUCTION

The Panzer – tank – was the vehicle which spearheaded the rapid German advance through Western Europe. Also the Panzer allowed the *Afrika Korps*, commanded by Erwin Rommel, to rapidly advance through the deserts of North Africa. The vehicles were deployed to lead the invasion of the Balkans and in the forefront of the invasion of Russia, advancing to the edge of Moscow. Panzers also led the attack on the Caucasus.

However, there is a danger of thinking that the stunning success of the German war machine in the first years of the war was due to this vehicle: this would be both wrong and imprecise. To completely understand the historical development in its entirety, it is wise to go back in history.

In 1915, during the catastrophe of World War I, infantry warfare came to a halt and opposing forces faced each other across a no-man's land. Modern weapons had entered the battlefield. New and accurate heavy artillery allowed a steady and precise bombardment of the front line. Here, among the hundred thousands of soldiers cowering in trenches, barbed-wire and the machine gun dominated the battlefield. For the next few years the battle was static; many times an advance was followed by an immediate retreat.

To breach this stalemate a new weapon was developed and appeared on the battlefront: The tank. Although the contribution it made to the Allied victory is commonly overestimated, it certainly marked the dawn of a new age in mobile warfare. By the end of the war an estimated 8,000 tanks had been produced.

The war ended in November 1918 with the unconditional surrender of the *Reich*. The German Empire had been defeated both economically and militarily. After the war the balance of power in Europe completely

Left:
German forces captured some 40 British Mk IV tanks on the Western Front. The tanks were transported to the *Bayerische-Armee-Kraftwagen* Park 20 (BAKP 20) workshop at Charleroi, Belgium, to be dismantled and repaired for return to the battlefront to fight against the British and French forces. (NARA)

Above:
Mechanics at BAKP 20 dismantle and inspect the drive units of a British Mk IV tank. The vehicle in the background has been painted in German-style camouflage and carries the German *Balkenkreuz*. The first combat using the *Beutepanzerwagen* (*Beute* – looted [captured]) was by *Sturmpanzer-Kraftwagen-Abteilung* in early 1918. (NARA)

changed; the monarchies of Germany, Austria-Hungary and Russia had been overthrown, and the Ottoman Empire had disintegrated. A new global player had entered the field: the United States of America.

A League of Nations was formed to prevent any armed international conflict and solve differences by diplomacy. A fragile peace followed until 1939.

However, after the end of the war further problems arose. The German *Reich* was held responsible for the war and the victors, mainly France, demanded immense reparations. Furthermore, the Treaty of Versailles forced the German *Reich* to disarm and abandon all overseas colonies. It is interesting that the German delegation was not allowed to participate in these negotiations.

Quite naturally, the content of the treaty was controversial. The French and others were not content, and judge the volume of the reparations as

being too low. However, the respected British economist Keynes thought that the terms of the treaty as being too harsh and counterproductive. Time would show that Keynes' fears were valid. In Germany, the conditions set out in the treaty, justified or not, were disputed and most unpopular. The rampant inflation in Germany, which had begun at the outbreak of World War I, reached a climax in 1923 after the French Occupation of the Ruhr, the largest industrial area in Germany. The population was severely affected and held the French occupiers responsible. The Great Depression, of the late 1920s, aggravated the situation. A high rate of unemployment and a depressed population prepared the ground for nationalism to rise unchallenged. In this atmosphere of desperation Hitler was able to seize the power, undermining and finally supplanting the fragile German democracy.

Above:
A rebuilt Mk IV of *Sturmpanzer-Kraftwagen-Abteilung* (*Beute*) parked on a street in Armentiéres, France shortly before the type was first used in combat by German forces during March 1918. Any success was limited due to the usage of inexperience crews and who had not been sufficiently trained in tank tactics. (NARA)

The army of 100,000

In the inter-war period the German military, hampered by the restrictions, maintained as a small standing army, the 100,000 *Mann-Heer* (army of 100,000 men), which was allowed to be used to maintain law and order in Germany. Thus the creation of the German tank force took place under most difficult circumstances, with all work cloaked in secrecy. The first tracked vehicles and tanks were developed as 'agricultural tractors' by companies like Daimler-Benz, Rheinmetall and Krupp. Testing the vehicles was possible only at locations a long distance from Germany. At that time the fledgling German republic was in close contact with the Soviet Union, which was most interested in all types of modern technology. The German prototypes could be tested without being observed in the eastern regions of Russia. It was here the trials to develop the combat methods for the new vehicles were first carried out.

Author's Note

I will try to explain the origin and development of the German tank force comprehensibly and accurately. Wherever possible, original German official documents have been referred to and all relevant technical data used. Thanks to the German bureaucratic mind many documents were created, and

Below:
The 30-ton A7V was the Germany's answer to British and French tank designs. Both countries produced more than 8,000 tanks, whereas Germany was only able to deliver 20 before the end of World War I. The A7V was armed with six machine guns and a 57mm main gun mounted at the front. (von Aufsess)

Above:
The four *Sturmpanzerwagen* A7V being unloaded near Charleroi, Belgium represent 20 percent of German tank production in World War I. Despite having a superior drive train, the A7V had an inferior cross-country performance to that of enemy tanks. (Kümmel)

Left:
Armoured cars were cheaper and simpler to manufacture than tanks, and both sides deployed significant numbers of the type during World War I. This Daimler DZVR 21 *Schützpolizei Sonderwagen* (police special vehicle), armed with two machine guns, was developed after the war. (Hoppe)

Above:
Officers and officials of the *Inspektion der Kraftfahrtruppen* (Inspectorate of Motorized Troops) photographed in 1933. Seated from the left are Walther Nehring and the two officers who are known as the founders of the *Panzerwaffe*, Oswald Lutz (centre) and Heinz Guderian (right). (Anderson)

subsequently stored. Luckily, many of these files survived the war and were collected by members of the Allied military. Much of this material has been archived at the National Archives and Records Administration (NARA) in Washington, DC. The original documents were returned to Germany, and are located at the Bundesarchiv-Militärarchiv in Freiburg. These sources are more or less available to the public, and have been used in my research for this book.

The nomenclature for German weapons, vehicles and tanks followed a clear structure. Tanks were *Panzerkampfwagen*, abbreviated to PzKpfw. The term *Sonderkraftfahrzeug* (SdKfz) for special purpose motor vehicle was also ubiquitous. This strict naming was possibly a result of a certain German, or Prussian tradition – discipline, precision and (sometimes) slavish obedience.

However, in service on the frontline a commanding officer would use a different designation than his technical officer. A PzKpfw IV, for

instance, was normally referred to only as the Panzer IV, or Pz IV. The production variants, commonly denoted as *Ausführung* (Ausf – model or mark) with letter (A, B, etc.) were absolutely irrelevant to him. Only the technical officer would have needed to know which model, and its chassis numbers. Matters changed when the long-barreled 5cm and 7.5cm guns were introduced. Subsequently, the terms *Langrohr* (Long barrel) and *Kurzrohr* (Short barrel) described the length. Now a clear differentiation was essential. But again, in his reports the unit commander would have used the simple suffixes k (*kurz*) and l (*lang*).

I will use the various designations as I found them in official reports, government orders, factory correspondence or, of greater importance, in the after action reports written by front-line commanders.

Thomas Anderson
June 2015

Above:
The Vickers Mk I light cavalry tank, was the backbone of the British army until the mid-1930s. The interesting design shows many characteristics of a modern tank, it mounted a 47mm main gun in a centrally-positioned rotatable turret. The type also carried no less than four machine guns. (Anderson)

CHAPTER 1

LAYING THE FOUNDATIONS

Heinz Guderian has always been seen as the 'father' of the German tank force. He was born in 1888, and served in a front-line signals battalion during World War I.

After the war he was selected for service in the Reichswehr and served briefly in Prussia, where he fought against Soviet forces menacing the fragile situation in the Baltic. After some years as an instructor at a military school in Stettin, he transferred to the motorized troops. This was an awakening for the ageing officer who maintained a youthful attitude to life. Guderian, who always showed a great interest in sophisticated technology and new tactics, finally had the opportunity to make a significant contribution to the transformation of the Reichswehr into a modern army. After the long years of comparatively easy tasks, this was a true challenge. His experiences in World War I had left the impression that due to the enormous firepower of modern artillery, conventional offensive operations would not be feasible in any future conflict. Conversely, he was certain that only the tank would be the decisive weapon on any future battlefield. However, Guderian also realized that this would apply only under very special conditions. He demanded speed for a successful breakthrough operation and the concentration of his attacking forces against a specific target to shatter the defensive lines of the enemy. The fast-moving armoured forces should then exploit this local success and fan out to enlarge the gap. By employing and developing these theories Guderian and a number of his staff officers began to elaborate tactics for the future, but at that time, a hypothetical German tank force.

Guderian wrote in his book:

Left:
Panzerkampfwagen I Ausf A being used by tank crews of 4.*Panzerdivision* to practice manoeuvring through forested areas at Modling training grounds, near Vienna, in May 1941. (Anderson)

Above:
The Krupp-built *Leichttraktor* was designed in the late 1920s, and was extensively tested at the *Panzerschule* (tank school) training grounds at Kazan in Soviet Russia. This is a later version with modified suspension and is fitted with a *Gefechtsantenne* (frame aerial) around the superstructure. The 8-ton vehicle mounted a 3.7cm gun and a *Machinengehwehr* 13k (MG 13k). (Anderson)

In 1929, I was finally convinced that Panzers could never play a decisive role if they are closely deployed with the infantry. My studies in military history, the evaluation of the large exercises in Great Britain and our own experiences with dummy tanks persuaded me that Panzers can exploit their extraordinary performance only if all associated support weapons, on whose assistance the Panzer relied, would be able to follow. Both speed and cross-country mobility of the respective forces have to be on a similar level. The Panzer must lead all other forces have to follow. We must not deploy Panzer within infantry divisions, and must establish *Panzerdivisionen*, which include all the support weapons required for a successful combat…

However in 1929, Guderian had to fight against many reservations uttered by senior German military leaders, who deemed such units as *Panzerdivisionen* as a dream. The *Reich* was surviving despite a severe economic crisis as the rate of unemployment increased.

In early 1930, Guderian was given command of *Kraftfahrabteilung* 3, a Prussian unit formed of four companies, stationed partly in Berlin and also Neisse/Lusatia. Guderian promptly started modifying this *Abteilung*

to his wishes.

The 1.*Kompanie* (Kp – Company) received Daimler Benz DZVR 21 *Schutzen Polezie-Sonderwagen* (police personal carrier) which entered service after World War I. The 4.Kp supported the 1.Kp with motor-cycles and was the only unit armed with machine guns. Together, both companies played the rôle of a *Panzeraufklärungs-Abteilung* (armoured reconnaissance battalion). The 2.Kp simulated the *Panzer-Kompanie*, and was equipped with dummy tanks. The 3. *Panzerabwehr-Kompanie* (tank destroyer company), was also provided with dummy guns.

It can be assumed that *Kraftfahrabteilung* 3 formed the nucleus of what would later become the *Panzerwaffe*. The unit was regularly ordered to participate in numerous military manoeuvres. But, Guderian always complained that most military authorities did not take him, or *Kraftfahrabteilung* 3 seriously. Due to the restrictions of the Treaty of Versailles, the German army was still not allowed to have tanks, and as most of the German military had never seen an operational tank in combat; Guderian's dummy tanks raised pitiful laughter.

By the spring of 1931, *Oberst* Oswald Lutz, was promoted to General

Above:
As the German military was not allowed to have tanks under the terms of the Treaty of Versailles they were forced to use *Panzerkampfwagen-Nachbildungen*, (dummy tanks) when on manoeuvres. Passenger vehicles like the BMX 'Dixi' (a British-designed Austin 7 built under licence in Germany) were fitted with a dummy. (Anderson)

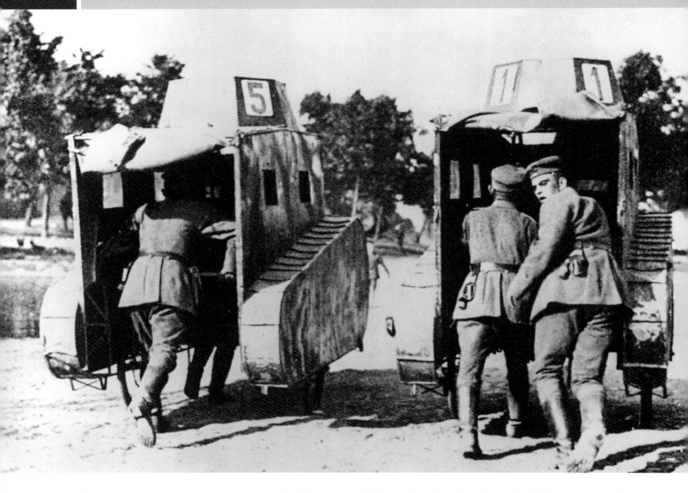

Above:
The first dummy tanks were mounted on frames fitted with bicycle wheels and had to be pushed over the 'battlefield'. For authenticity the 'tanks' were painted with tactical markings for this exercise in 1927. (bpk)

and succeeded Otto von Stülpnagel as the *Inspekteur der Verkehrstruppen* 6 (In.6 – inspector of motorized troops). Guderian appreciated that his direct superior had good organizational skills and, for his age, a surprising understanding of technical matters. General Lutz supported Guderian´s ideas and together they formed the organizational background for the future German armoured forces.

Of similar importance, however, was the theoretical background which was compiled by Guderian and his staff.

In his book Guderian mentions a simple numbers game:

Red and Blue wage war against each other. Each party has 100 infantry divisions and 100 tank battalions. Red has deployed its tanks in the infantry divisions: Blue combined them with divisions as army troops. Over a front of 300km we assume 100km being safe against mechanized warfare, a further 100km being difficult to negotiate by tanks, and 100km suited for tank attacks. For an attack the following scenario is likely: Red has disposed a considerable part of its tanks in more or less impassable terrain, where they cannot move forward. A further part of the Red tank force will be hindered by difficult terrain. Thus Red has only a small part of its tanks in the sector with favourable terrain available. On the contrary, Blue has concentrated its tank force where they want to press for a victory, and where a commitment of tanks is possible. Here Blue can attack with a double superiority, while the rest of its tanks are available elsewhere to defend possible counterstrikes…

Thus a decision to evenly disperse the tank force to infantry divisions will be a step back to the primitive British tactics of 1916/17, which at that time totally failed. It was not until Cambrai that their concentrated commitment of tanks led to a convincing success…

After World War I, a firm conviction prevailed that, despite the experience at Cambrai, the artillery and specialized anti-tank weapons would be able to stop any tank assault. Among many army officers and civilian administrators, be it home or abroad, an opinion was formed that any capital spending on large tank forces would be a waste.

Not surprisingly, Guderian and his staff disagreed with this opinion. The tank assaults in the final period of World War I had been thoroughly analyzed, as were the few available reports provided by Ernst Volckheim (by 1918 *Leutnant*), a commander of a German A7V tank. In the meantime, Guderian made visits to a number of foreign tank units, among these to the Swedish Army, where he gained valuable experience.

His organizational structures had to be different to all of those units he had visited in Britain and France, both of which maintained large armoured forces.

At the end of the 1920s, Britain, France and the Soviet Union intensified their efforts to build up their armoured forces. As noted in a German document dated April 1937, the basic combat principles of these possible future opponents were as follows:

Since the end of the war the European armies have chosen different ways regarding the tactical advancement of their tank forces.
France defines the true determination of her tank formations in the direct and immediate consolidation of the attack power of the infantry.
England does not integrate her tanks into the infantry to the same degree as France. However, tanks have to assist other weapons, especially the infantry. The main task of British tank units is the exploitation of any battle success, and the participation in rapid operations, which require speed and great operating range.
Finally, Russia follows both methods: the French tight coupling of tanks and infantry as well as a disengaged and far more independent commitment…

Seen in retrospect this assessment, written in 1937, was very close to reality.

However, it is uncertain whether Guderian and his staff were able to forecast or recognize this development as early as the end of the 1920s, when the nucleus of the future *Panzerwaffe* was theoretically discussed. In Germany, at that time, neither the tanks had been produced nor had the organizational structures been decided. In summary, the German military had to admit to be entering into the unknown. But the dummy tanks played an important rôle in this period allowing infantry to gain experience of operating with a 'mechanized' force.

In 1932, In.6 organized a field exercise in which a large number of *Kampfwagen-Nachbildung* (KpfwNachbBtn – dummy tank battalions) were involved. After the event a report detailing the results of the important exercise was written. Excerpt:

Suggestions and lessons learned from the joint exercises with the dummy tank battalions in cooperation with infantry and artillery forces at the Grafenwöhr and Jüterbog training areas.

Purpose of the exercises:
a) Clarification of the theories on tank tactics
b) Exercise and experience concerning anti-tank defense
c) Exercise and experiences of cooperation of tanks and other weapons
d) Collection of experiences of leadership during mobile exercises

As for a)
2)
The tank is an exclusively attack weapon and will be used in focal points to make a breakthrough. Wherever they will be used, they will temporarily be the main and most important weapon.
3)
Tank units will receive independent combat orders with special consideration of their high firepower and mobility. Any commitment to less mobile units has to be refused, as their advantages will be diminished.
4)
Tank units can therefore never be a subordinated part of the infantry.
5)
Any deployment of tanks under battalion strength has to be rejected. A sole company cannot gain a decisive success facing the qualities of known anti-tank weapons.
6)
For a successful commitment of tanks the element of surprise will be the most important advantage.
8)
A succession of tanks in several waves has proved to be most favourable.
12)

The place of the tank battalion commander has to be in the forefront of the attack, to quickly react on changing conditions.
13)
Commanding a tank unit requires high mental agility and guile. Quick decisions have to be made and promptly acted upon. Field orders are the rule…
14)
Upon reaching its objectives, the company or platoon leader has to re-launch the attack, or turn the attack to any flank and take advantage of the achieved breakthrough.
17)
The requirement for a platoon of light tanks for the staff of the tank battalion is a proven necessity. These tanks are important for reconnaissance duties, and for the liaison with the tank companies and other units…
As for d)

Below:
A dummy tank built on the chassis of a Hanomag 2/10PS passenger car to resemble a French tank of that period. (Hoppe)

Above:
The Daimler-Benz version of the *Grosstraktor* (also built by Rheinmetall-Borsig) mounted a 7.5cm gun and three *Maschinengewehr* 13k. One was mounted in a small turret at the rear of the vehicle, typical for tanks designed in the early 1930s. The gun on this vehicle has been removed from the armoured mantlet. (Anderson)

1) Due to the lack of radio equipment many problems regarding the leading of the KpfwNachbBtl occurred…

2) The speed of the tank force … calls for a rapid advance in the course of the battle.

After Hitler seized power, General Lutz issued a further statement on 3 August 1933 in which he described the fundamental problems his fledgling force had to face:

Expansion of motorized combat elements

Other armies are equipped with modern firearms, while the attack power of our armed forces has diminished since 1914. After 1919 [Versailles] the German *Reichsheer* had to be established according to this treaty, and without heavy weapons it has no attack power at all. Facing her neighbours equipped with new and modern aircraft, tanks and heavy artillery, the *Reichsheer* has only weak defence force. The imposed limitations make even a defensive war hopeless…

I however, believe that I have to make some suggestions… These are stated in the armed forces´ office development programme:

Most important is the requirement for utmost operational mobility. This is because we have to compensate for our numerical inferiority. Only operational mobility will ensure freedom of action… Besides fully exploiting the railway network and motorized transport on roads, this operative mobility can only be achieved by quick mobile combat elements, which can be used independently from other forces against the flanks and rear of the enemy. This task cannot be accomplished by the cavalry anymore… This task can only be fulfilled by motorized combat elements… Tank forces will make the decisive breakthrough, with speed and firepower, the following light divisions [in this context infantry forces subordinated to the tank division, author] will only have to exploit the situation…

For the realization of the above mentioned measures I suggest:
1) Tank units in liaison with light divisions. Due to the absence of own research, we have to rely on experiences made by foreign countries, which cannot be fully verified. Therefore we have to build up our own formations step-by-step, incorporating foreign experience, and the work of our own *Versuchsverbänden* (experimental units). Independent from this, the establishmnet of tank battalions in the future is indispensable.

Suggestion:

• Establishment of seven tank battalions in regiments of two to three battalions each…
• Establishment of a motorized-rifle battalion

2) Advancement of the motorized-recconnaissance battalion.
3) Reinforcement of the number of tank destroyer companies
4) The enhancement of the tactical mobility of the further subordinated units…

b)
For the newly to be established tank unit (including light division) in the first instance, a regiment staff has to be formed, which will be directly subordinated under the *Inspekteur* [Lutz]. Later this staff will be developed to a brigade staff, which will immediately start the preparations for the experimental unit to be established in 1935…

This was the starting point for the first German armoured formation, the 1.*Panzerdivision*. In October 1934, important decisions were finalized and the first machine-gun armed tank delivered.

Above:
A line of dummy tanks (which have the appearance of a British Army Vickers cavalry tank) built on the chassis of the BMW 'Dixi', give fire support to machine-gun teams as they prepare to move forward and attack the 'enemy' during an exercise in 1928. (bpk)

Panzerwaffe – genesis of the hardware

The tank was designed and developed as the weapon to break the 'stalemate' of trench warfare in World War I. It is still difficult to determine as to how important the Allied tank force was in the final outcome of World War I. One matter appears to be clear, the German military (and industry) were taken by surprise and their development of the tank continued without any urgency.

However, German forces used some 200 captured British Mk IV tanks as *Beutepanzer* until the end of the war. The first German tank, *Sturmpanzerwagen* A7V, entered service in 1918, but only twenty were produced. A few battle reports have been published. In his most interesting, if somewhat one-sided book, Major Ernst Volckheim, the commander of an A7V, describes the German tank as being superior to its British counterparts. However, the author wishes to point out that this book was written in 1937 and is based on the personal recollections of Volckheim:

> In contrast to the layout of the enemy tanks the tracks of the A7V-*Sturmpanzerwagenagen* were protected by armour plates. The fact that each track was powered by one engine resulted in a better steering performance. Due to the thicker armour, vulnerability to enemy fire was lower. On the other hand the mobility of the A7V in rugged terrain, under constant artillery fire, was significantly worse. Trenches and shell craters

caused serious problems. The strong armour protection (30mm at the front, 16mm at the sides and 20mm at the rear) offered sufficient protection against infantry fire. The heavy German tank was even safe against hits from armour-piercing rounds…

…The British *Beutekampfwagen* (improved Mk IV), which were used by Germany, had a clearly weaker fighting power than the A7V. Due to the exposed tracks and the weaker armour protection, the tank was vulnerable to infantry fire. Driver and commander were placed in the front of the vehicle. While the driver operated the engine and the transmission, the commander had to handle the steering brakes to initiate turns… Orders were shouted. The commander had no influence on the firing of the weapons; he was occupied guiding the tank by operating the steering brakes. The commander's observation was limited; he had no view to the sides…

Volckheim finished this chapter in his book with a more or less helpless, but patriotric conclusion:

Despite the many disadvantages of the *Beutekampfwagen* we had been able to gain many great successes. These positive results were gained owing to the abilities of the commanders and the competence of the crews rather than to the technical perfection of the [British] tanks.

Below:
Adolf Hitler and his entourage attend the first major exercise undertaken by 1.PzDiv in 1935. Five *Grosstraktoren* are lined up for the presentation, all are 7.5cm armed test vehicles. (Anderson)

German industry had a skilled workforce available – Germany was one of the leading industrial powers in the world – but the situation in the inter-war period was not favourable. In 1930, many parts of the German armaments industry were still restricted, and mistrust was rife. The severe restrictions of the Treaty of Versailles had officially banned any overt work in this field, and also the acquisition of heavy armaments including tanks.

Quite naturally, the German government sought options to secretly by-pass these restrictions and tanks were considered as being most important for the building of a strong army in the future.

The Germans followed all international military developments with interest. As stated earlier, the developed nations (Britain, France, Soviet Union, and the USA) did not make heavy investments the modernization of their armed forced directly after World War I. Nevertheless, their armament industries did produce prototype vehicles and weapons and sought customers around the world.

In the mid-1920s, the British army had disbanded their original tank units. The Royal Tank Regiment (RTR) was equipped with 200 Vickers Medium tanks, a modern design armed with a 47mm gun in a large rotatable turret. The Vickers Company continued with the development of the tank and produced the Vickers Mk E, or 'Six-Ton Tank'. Although not adopted for service by the British, this light tank set the standard for many future designs. The Soviet Union acquired a licence for the type and improved the design to produce the T-26 tank. This tank was truly massed produced with over 10,000 built. Further customers which purchased a licence to produce Vickers designs were Poland and also the Czech Republic.

After Vickers acquired Carden-Loyd, the company produced a number of different tankettes. The Carden-Loyd suspension system, due to the rugged construction, reliability and cost effectiveness, was produced under licence by many nations – including the German *Reich*.

Vickers developed another interesting vehicle, the Vickers 'Independent'. This heavy tank weighed 30 tons, and was fitted with a main turret mounting a 47mm gun and another four turrets mounting light machine guns. However, neither the British government nor any other nation was interested in buying this tank. Despite this, the multi-turret design appears to have inspired tank designers worldwide, among them France, Germany and, again, the Soviet Union. The latter was the only nation to produce their designs, the T-28 and T-35 in larger numbers.

Early German developments

In 1927, Daimler-Benz, Krupp and Rheinmetall were commissioned to develop a modern heavy tank armed with a 7.5cm gun. The secret project had the codename *Grosstraktor* (heavy tractor), and each company produced two vehicles very similar in design. The main armament was mounted in a turret: a second turret mounting a machine gun was installed towards the rear of the vehicle.

Above:
The PzKpfw I Ausf A,
SdKfz 101
(*Sonderkraftfahrzeug* –
special-purpose vehicle)
was a small vehicle and
had a two-man crew.
It was armed with two
Maachinengewehr 13k
mounted in a rotatable
turret. By 1940, most
PzKpfw I Ausf A had been
withdrawn from front-line
units. (Anderson)

A year later, a light tank armed with a 3.7cm gun was ordered. Krupp and Rheinmetall delivered two examples each and the type was designated as the *Leichttraktor* (light tractor).

In the 1920s, tank manufacturers were learning how to design tanks by experience. In Germany there were only few engineers sufficiently experienced in the design and manufacture of tank transmission, steering and suspension – they were working in uncharted waters.

Since the British, French and US governments remained suspicious of German militarism, a strange collaboration far in the east was initiated. The new German republic sought assistance in the Soviet Union and subsequently a test facility was established at Kazan, 600km east of Moscow. On completion, the prototypes were transported to Kama for development trials. It is obvious that both sides gained from this cooperation.

The time spent at *Panzerschule* (tank school) Kazan was of essential importance to the German tank industry. The vehicles were thoroughly tested under all conditions and all components underwent a detailed examination. New technology, including radio telegraphy, was also tested under battlefield conditions. The course for the coming German arms build-up was set. At the same time the first officers of the emerging *Panzertruppe* were trained for this new, sophisticated type of warfare.

By December 1932, the German *Reich* had achieved full military equality. When Hitler came to power, all cooperation with the Soviet Union came to an end and *Panzerschule* Kama was subsequently closed.

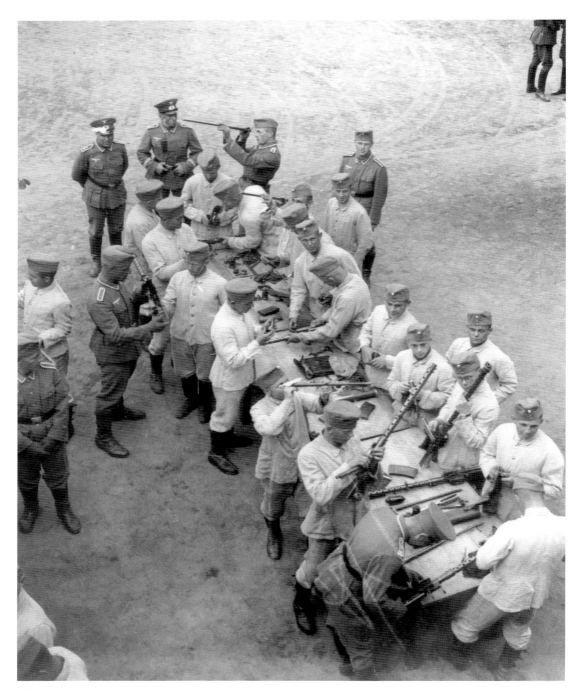

Above:
Regular care and maintenance was of great importance: *Panzermänner* (tank crews) are taught to clean their machine guns under the watchful eyes of their instructors. One is cleaning a standard longer-barreled MG 13k. (NARA)

General considerations – the gear for the coming conflict

While both the *Leichttraktor* and the *Grosstraktor* were being tested at Kama, *Waffenprüfämet* 6 (WaPrüf 6 – Weapons Testing Department) demanded the development of a new medium tank. The specification for this *mittlerer Traktor* (medium tractor) was set in 1932 and differed from earlier types. The main turret mounted two main weapons, a 7.5cm and a 3.7cm gun. Two smaller machine-gun (MG) turrets were mounted to the front and at the rear of the fighting compartment. Similar to previous vehicles the tracks were driven by rear sprockets.

The *mittlerer Traktor* was designated as the *Neubaufahrzeug* (NbFz), and set the standard for the future German main-battle tank. Five test vehicles were built, two from mild steel, three from rolled (armoured) steel.

The 3.7cm *Kampfwagenkanone* (KwK) was a multi-purpose gun designed and developed by Rheinmetall-Borsig at their factory in Düsseldorf. The gun was chosen as it was also intended to be used for the 3.7cm *Tankabwehrkanone* (TaK – anti-tank gun) for the proposed *Panzerabwehrkompanien* (anti-tank companies).

The 7.5cm KwK was designed as a fire-support weapon as it fired a destructive high-explosive (HE) round.

Above:
An instructor illustrates the trajectory of gunfire and the relevant telescopic sight markings on a blackboard during ballistic training for the company. (NARA)

It is interesting to note that while the production of the *Neubaufahrzeug* was underway, it was already being considered to replace the gun the 3.7cm gun with a heavier 5cm gun when it became available. Perhaps this was a hint of early doubts, in the German military, as to the effectiveness of the 3.7cm gun?

However, the plans for the proposed *Panzerdivisionen* required large numbers of armoured vehicles – tanks. Due to financial restrictions and technical problems, it was decided to introduce a light tank first.

From *Kampfwagentruppe* to *Panzertruppe*

In January 1935, General Lutz made further proposals for the deployment of armoured units. On 22 January, the *Chef der Heeresleitung*, Freiherr von Fritsch, asked some pertinent questions. Excerpt:

> a) Are we able, and should we establish further divisional staffs?
> c) How long will the complete establishment take?
> d) When will the motorized troops be combat ready…

General Lutz's office answered promptly:

> As for a)
> The establishment of divisional staffs for the *Panzerdivisionen* in the autumn of 1935 is absolute essential to give the newly-formed troops the necessary leadership…
> As for c)
> The equipment with material for the training will take place upon establishment. The 5. and 6. PzRgt can be provided with ten *MG-Kampfwagen* (training vehicles) per company.
> As for e)
> The 1. and 2. PzDiv will be provided with *MG-Kampfwagen* by 1 April 1936, the 3. PzDiv will follow half a year later. In April 1937, the divisions will be endued with 140 *Kampfwagen* 3.7 cm and 10 *Kampfwagen* 7.5 cm…

However, these proposed numbers were unrealistic. In 1936, a chart detailing productions statistics was published. The target numbers for 3.7cm and 7.5cm armed tanks proved to almost impossible for German industry to produce.

General Lutz department had also to deal with serious problems in terms of personnel:

> A.) Motorized-combat units
>
> The deployment of the proposed three *Panzerdivisionen* and three further *Panzerbrigaden* shall be accelerated… To enable the deployment, a

police unit shall be drawn on… *Polizei-Regiment* 'Brandenburg' will form one *Panzerdivision*. Four anti-tank battalions of the *Reichsheer* will be ordered to establish four Panzer battalions with three companies each…

In accordance with this the following picture emerges:

1. *Panzerdivision* (Berlin)

Stab PzDiv 1	Divisional staff	Berlin
Stab PzBrig 1	Brigade staff	Potsdam
Pz Regiment 1	1. Tank Rgt	Wünsdorf
Pz Regiment 3	3. Tank Rgt	Neuruppin
Schützenregiment 1	1. Inf Rgt	Brandenburg
Aufklärungsabteilung	Recce Bn	Stahnsdorf
Panzerabwehrabteilung	Tank Destroyer Bn	Wünsdorf
Artillerie Regiment 1	Artillery Rgt 1	Eberswalde, Neuruppin
Pionier Kompanie	Engineer Co	Hannoversch-München
Div *Nachrichten* Abt	Div Signals Bn	Stahnsdorf…

Above:
The German army attached great importance to reliable radio contact between a battalion and the company and also between the company leader and the tanks under his command. Dedicated command tanks were built and issued to tank companies and battalions at staff level. The *kleiner Panzerbefehlswagen* (k PzBflWg) was built on the chassis of the PzKpfw I Ausf A and fitted with a fixed superstructure. (Anderson)

The 2. and 3. *Panzerdivisionen* were established in sequence. Despite the many problems, Lutz decided that three *Panzerdivisionen* were to be completely established by October and November 1935.

By the middle of the year, the German *Reich* declared full military sovereignty.

Despite General Lutz having a clear vision as to the tasks facing the future tank force; in 1936 there were still differing views about these questions. The *Allgemeines Heeresamt* (General Army Office), which was in charge of the *Ersatzheer* (replacement and training army) stated on 22 January 1936:

The main task of the tank was and will be the assistance of the infantry assault…

A week later, the chief of the *Generalstab des Heeres* (GenStbH – general staff of the army), General Beck, an artillery officer, distinctly contradicted and clarified his view on the requirements put to future tank formations:

Tank units
The support of the infantry attack is one of the tasks of the tank force. This view is backed by observing nations with greater experience. However, for the technical equipment and the organization of tank units we have to put our full

Below:
When production of the PzKpfw I Ausf B began a larger command variant was developed. Designated, *Panzerbefehlswagen* I (SdKfz 265), it provided more space for the radio equipment. This vehicle is fitted with a non-standard frame aerial and was used for radio-range extension tests. (Anderson)

emphasis on combat with enemy tanks: combat against living targets and enemy anti-tank guns are secondary… Against modern enemy tanks with 25mm armour plate, a calibre of 3.7cm is required. So I must insist on my demand to mount at least 66 percent of the tanks of the light companies with the 3.7cm TaK… This will give our troops a morale boost, which will be needed to fulfil their tasks. Higher asset and maintenance costs have to be accepted.

In mid-1936 the GenStbH continued:

To the Commander-in-Chief of the Army

1) After disbandment of the cavalry and under consideration of the offensive capacities of a modern army, the mechanized formations have to adopt two fields of duty. Their equipment has to be adapted accordingly:

a) Deployment as the decisive attack or penetration force:
• Frontal attack in cooperation with the other large formations
• Completion of the penetration to a breakthrough
• Assault against the flanks…

Above:
Oberstleutnant Spannenkrebs, the commander of PzRgt 3 in his PzKpfw I Ausf A during late 1936. At that time the unit was equipped only with PzKpfw I and II. Even in August 1939, immediately before beginning of the attack on Poland, the regiment had only three PzKpfw III and ten PzKpfw IV available. (Anderson)

Above:
Tanks of PzRgt 2 lined up in the area outside the garrison in Eisenach, Thuringia. The PzKPfw I was inexpensive to produce which allowed the establishment of large armoured formations. (NARA)

b) Deployment in terms of duties performed by the old cavalry
- Reconnaissance duties in front of the army or the main line of defence including combat against enemy reconnaissance or forward forces
- Rapid occupation of vital sectors
- Surrounding and overtaking of enemy forces

2) … The fulfillment of the tasks shown under 1a, are by today´s standards the condition for the success of any assault. Thus the suitability for combat against enemy artillery and tank formations is absolutely necessary. Thus a greater firepower and adequate protection against enemy fire must be demanded… The main weapon will be the PzKpfw with armour-piercing gun…

… In contrast to this, the tasks shown under 1b require formations with greater mobility and speed. The commitment against enemy tanks will be less likely… Thus armed with light tanks or all-terrain armoured cars will be sufficient.

3) … As a result of these ideas we assert that the different duties for above mentioned cannot be solved by a unit formation. Thus we must strive for:
- Heavy mechanized formations (PzDiv) for the duties shown under 1a.
- Light mechanized formations (le Div) for the duties under 1b.

Even by mid-1936, there were still divergent views as to the operational purpose of the *Panzerwaffe*. A letter from the GenStabH reveals:

Subject: Infantry tanks

1) Due to the experiences made in the [Great] war, by all nations, the technical development of tanks has been focused on an increase in speed and operational range. A higher speed and mobility will give tanks a higher survivability against modern anti-tank weapons than an increase of the armour with all its disadvantages (reduced speed, limited bridge crossing ability, and problematic transport during operational transfers.) With this process the tanks lost the ability to keep contact with the infantry…

2) We strive for a 66 percent share of 3.7cm armed tanks per battalion. In relation its armour protection this tank cannot fight in steady close cooperation with the infantry. In contrast to the walking speed of an advancing infantry tank, the fast 3.7cm tank will operate in wavelike deployment with all forces. By exact thoughtful planning a steady support of the infantry in the zone of resistance will be assured…

Below:
During the establishment of the *Panzerwaffe* in the mid-1930s, tanks were still treated as a special vehicle. New recruits examine this PzKpfw I Ausf A of I./PzRgt 4 in a maintenance area, especially the Krupp M 304 Boxer-type. The tank carries a civilian license plate, very uncommon on a German tank. (NARA)

Above:
A company of PzKpfw I (LaS) supported by three Henschel Hs122 B-o aircraft of the *Luftwaffe*, advances towards 'enemy' positions during an exercise in 1937. (Hoppe)

3) The armour thickness will find its limitations, while the calibre of the main gun can be increased much easier. The heavily-armoured infantry tank, rather than the agile 3.7cm tank, will be exposed to the fire of enemy anti-tank guns

4) Furthermore, it will take four to five years of development, until a new infantry tank will be ready for production.

For these reasons Abt 2, GenStbdH considers a specialized tank for the direct support of the infantry as neither desired nor necessary.

Thus both the technical design and the tactical planning for the tank types to be introduced were clear by 1936. In the same year, GenStbH and In.6 agreed and issued a mutual statement:

1) Production of *Panzerwagen* will be prioritized to types with armour-piercing weapons (for the present 3.7cm).

Below:
This table shows the official target figures for the production and deployment of light MG (LaS) and 2cm (LaS 100) armed tanks, and also the heavier 3.7cm (ZW) and 7.5cm (BW) armed tanks.

Establishment of the *Kampfwagen truppe*	MG and 2cm armed PzKpfw		3.7cm armed PzKpfw		7.5cm armed PzKpfw	
October 1936	Number	Total MG/2cm	Number	Total 3.7cm	Number	Total 7.5cm
Brigade Staffs (4)	20		4			
Regimental Staffs (8)	40		24			
Battalions (16)	320		3816		208	
	(380)	380	(844)	844	(208)	208
October 1937						
Brigade Staff (1)	5		1			
Regimental Staffs (2)	10		6			
Battalions (8)	160		408		104	
	(175)	555	(415)	1,259	(104)	312
October 1938						
Brigade Staffs (2)	10		3			
Regimental Staffs (4)	20		12			
Battalions (12)	240		612		156	
	(270)	825	(626)	1,885	(156)	468
October 1939						
Brigade Staffs (2)	10		3			
Regimental Staffs (4)	20		12			
Battalions (12)	240		612		156	
	(270)	1,095	(626)	2,511	(156)	624
Reserve (25 percent)		274		628		156
Total		**1,369**		**3,139**		**780**

CHAPTER 2

THE FIRST
PANZERDIVISION

Germany, unlike France and Britain, had gained no experience fighting a battle using armoured formations. Therefore it is understandable that at all levels, bureaucrats, active officers and supply officials were discussing as how such a force should be assembled and effectively organized. Parts of this slow, but creative decision making were noted down in thousands of documents. Any evaluation of these is very difficult as many of these ideas were short-lived and not progressed any further

Organizational structures before the outbreak of war

When Guderian detailed an organizational plan for the proposed tank units, he had to work against strong resistance, but he also had some influential patrons. Werner Freiherr von Fritsch, Commander-in-Chief of the Army, supported Guderian and his ideas despite being considered to be most conservative in his views.

However, *Generaloberst* Ludwig Beck doggedly opposed these ideas, insisting that tanks should remain under the control of the infantry and that the largest organizational unit of the *Panzerwaffe* should be the brigade.

Beside his fundamental problem of being provided with insufficient funds, for tanks and support weapons, Guderian's vision was twofold.

His *Panzerdivision* should combine an armour component – tanks – with a strong infantry force. Thus the integral *Panzerbrigade* was to be reinforced by a *Schützenbrigade* (rifle brigade). The beauty of this idea lies in the shortcomings of the independent tank brigade. While the armoured formation could certainly make a decisive breakthrough, it lacked

Left:
A training exercise involving a PzKpfw I Ausf B with pioneer troops who have bridged a stream by using heavy timbers. (NARA)

Right:
A LaS 100, or PzKpKw II of 2.PzDiv, leads a parade through Vienna shortly after the *Anschluss* (annexation) of Austria to the *Reich* on 14 March 1938. The tank carries no markings as a system had not been established, which makes exact identification very difficult. (Münch)

Below:
All *Panzer-Abteilung* were issued with a large number of driver-training vehicles. These *Fahrschulwannen* used the PzKpfw I hull without the turret and superstructure. Here drivers test their skills on the 'Panzer-rocker'. (Münch)

Left:
In the years before outbreak of the war thousands of tank crews, especially drivers were trained in secret to ensure the number of personnel required for the formation of the planned *Panzerdivisionen* was available. (Historyfacts)

integrated elements to exploit the success and to hold the gained terrain. An integrated and highly coordinated *Panzerdivision* could perform defined missions with a greater chance of success.

However, Guderian also worked hard to make the concept of the *Panzerdivision* faster moving, faster reacting and harder hitting. His ambitious goal for the future of his new force was to see it equipped with modern multi-role tanks.

Testing the concept

The first *Panzerdivision* was established between 18 and 30 August 1935, at Münster in the Lüneburger Heide region of Germany and was immediately involved in a large field exercise at the site. The purpose of the exercise was to evaluate the tactics, organization and armament of large-scale tank formations. The exercise involved an estimated 13,000 soldiers, 4,000 motorized vehicles and 481 armoured vehicles.

It appears that all available tanks, even the few *Versuchsfahrzeuge* produced at the end of the 1920s, took part in this exercise. The majority, however, were machine-gun-armed LaS tanks (later named PzKpfw I). The existing *Grosstraktoren* and *Neubaufahrzeuge* simulated the heavy company.

Above:
A column of PzKpfw I
travel on a dirt track
in the farmland which
surrounded the Münster
training grounds. (NARA)

The following objectives for the exercise were stated:

1) Attack from the march without assembling
2) Large-scale march in darkness, followed by occupation of assembly positions at night and surprise attack at dawn.
3) Surprise attack from assembly positions

And, within the scope of cooperation with other forces

4) Commitment in the focal point of a battlezone to accomplish the break through.

The following observations were noted:

The March:
a)
Since tank units have to converge quickly and efficiently, a grouping of these units with slower forces is not possible…

e)

The maximum marching speed (average) is 18kph for tracked vehicles, 25kph for wheeled vehicles and 35kph for motorcycles…

Attack:

a) Preliminary notice:

At present the tank regiments are provided only with MG-armed tanks. During the exercise some older *Versuchsstücke* (3.7cm and 7.5cm tanks) were used as a heavy company. The combat against enemy tanks; be it in cooperation with infantry (as we can expect with French forces) or in greater formations, was not the purpose of the exercise… Initially the provision with a certain number of 2cm and 3.7cm armed tanks for every company is planned. Each battalion will be provided with one company of 7.5cm armed tanks…

Technical Experiences

1) The performance of motorized vehicles and their mobility is good…

a) During the exercise the following vehicles took part.

4,025 wheeled vehicles, of which 92 failed temporarily due to technical reasons = 2.3 percent

481 tanks, of which 27 failed temporarily due to technical reasons = 5.6 percent

Below:
The LaS, possibly the company leader's, in the foreground carries a small pennant marked with a geometric symbol, no other markings were used. Marked pennants are known to have been used by PzRgt 1 and 2 of 1.PzDiv. (Anderson)

Right:
An assault exercise using tanks; in the background is a purposely-built Potemkin-style village. Realistic exercises were and are still the basic training for any army. (Anderson)

The low percentage of failed wheeled and tracked vehicles is a result of the fact that many were new. Furthermore the temporary workshops worked well and efficiently, minor damages were repaired overnight...

5) Fuelling tankers under war conditions has to be basically improved. The large fuel vehicles, possibly with trailer, are too heavy and bulky and vulnerable to enemy fire. Their wartime usage on the frontline is impossible. The introduction of petrol carrying vehicles, with 20 litre cans, is advisable...

Possibly of greater importance was the evaluation of the used tactics. The report continues:

Experiences and thoughts on the usage of tank units:

1) In the course of the experimental exercise it was proven that a tank formation can fulfill all given tasks.

2) Two methods of application became apparent:
a) Independent combat
b) Combat in close cooperation with other units.

3) For decisive tasks within the scope of an army, their fighting power seems to be too low. According to the opinion of the *Kommando der Panzertruppen*, a reinforcement of the division is not the solution because the unit would become too unwieldy, and would lose its mobility and

agility. Instead a consolidation of several divisions to corps seems to be the solution.

4) The task of carry the attacking infantry can be solved by *Panzerbrigaden*. However, any operational exploitation of this success is not possible. *Panzerdivisionen* offer far more versatile possibilities. In emergencies its own *Panzerbrigaden* can immediately assist the infantry.

Experiences and thoughts about organization and equipment

According to previous experiences the organization and structure of a *Panzerdivision* has fulfilled our expectations. A final conclusion cannot be given, the test period was too short, the exercises too limited...

Below:
A view through the driver's visor of a LaS, or PzKpfw I, the armoured-glass vision blocks have been removed to allow a clearer view and better ventilation. (NARA)

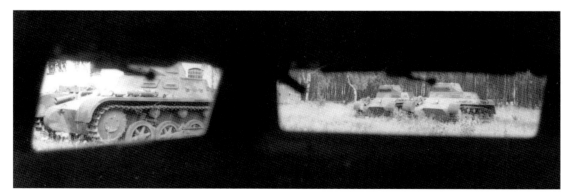

Above:
An LaS from PzRgt 3. The rhombus was coloured and possibly painted on a slightly darker rectangle. The colour of the rhombus denoted the *Kompanie* (1.Kp; white: 2.Kp; red: 3.Kp; yellow). (Münch)

Right:
Although hardly perceptible, the LaS to the right has a different camouflage scheme and appears to have been painted with the hard-edge style *Reichswehr Buntfarbenanstrich* (a multi-coloured coating of brown, green and sand yellow). (Historyfacts)

Above:
Two LaS of an unknown unit move up past a 7.5cm *Feldkanone* during one of the first field exercises. Due to the hot summer weather, the crew has opened the engine hatches to improve cooling. The crew manning the field gun is wearing old-style *Reichswehr* steel helmets. (NARA)

Left:
A line of LaS is parked on an open field, as their commander's wait for the order to advance. (NARA)

1) Demands
a) *Panzerregimenter*
The present provision of MG tanks is a stop gap solution. A quick integration with tanks fitted with armour-piercing guns and a number of 7.5cm armed tanks are absolutely necessary. Following these demands the *Abteilung* must be arranged as follows:

Three light companies with MG-armed tanks, mixed with armour-piercing gun tanks.
One heavy company with 7.5cm armed tanks.

b) For the leader of a *Panzerdivision* and a *Panzerbrigade*: *Führerkampfwagen* [command tanks] with wireless equipment are essential ...

c) A light tank platoon for the staff of a *Panzerbrigade*, as is already provided for the staffs of PzRgt and PzAbt... Will offer immediate protection of the brigade leader in combat... Furthermore reconnaissance missions can achieved when require by the light tank platoon at any time ...

d) The staff sections of the *Schützenbrigade*, the *Schützenregiment*, the *Schützenbataillone*, the motor-cycle battalion, the reconnaissance battalion,

Below:
This rear view of an LaS, clearly shows that good observation for the crew was an essential part of German tank design; note the visor slots. The use of a playing card symbol indentifies this vehicle as being from 2.PzDiv. (NARA)

and the artillery and pioneers have to be provided with armoured vehicles (command tanks with wireless)...

e) The *Schützenbrigade*, the *Schützenregiment* and the *Schützenbataillone* must be provided with *Panzerspähzüge* (armoured reconnaissance platoons)...

f) An artillery regimental staff and a second artillery battalion with three batteries of 10.5cm l FH 18 *Feldhaubitze* (field howitzer)...

g) The tank destroyer battalion has to be reinforced from nine to twelve guns per company...

h) Provision of the signals battalion with armoured vehicles...

The report culminates in further perceptions:

a) Speed and agility are the preconditions for the successful commitment of a *Panzerdivision*. Accordingly, they must consist of manageable BUT not too large units, whose mobility is to be assured by releasing all subunits not necessary for the success...

Above:
The crews of a column of LaS in a *leichte Panzerkompanie*, take a break in a tree-lined lane to avoid the summer heat of 1936. They are wearing the distinctive black *Sonderbekleidung für Kampfwagenbesatzungen* (special clothing for armoured vehicle crews). (Historyfacts)

Above:
Reichsparteitag, Zeppelinfeld! On the occasion of the NSDAP party congress 1936 the first mass parade of tanks was performed – a powerful symbol of Hitler's pretension to power. The morale impact of tanks and airplanes in the absolutely tasteless stone desert of the Nazi party rally grounds in Nuremberg must have been impressive. (Anderson)

b) For the organization of a *Panzerdivision* there are essentially two different perceptions possible. One agrees to the earlier valid structures, the other suggests dedicated tank and infantry units which are not combined in a division assembly....

d) The question of dividing the *Panzerbrigade* into three *Abteilungen* will have to be examined in the near future... Dividing the brigade in three subunits will improve the agility of the *Panzerbrigade*...

Different points of view remained between the decision makers. In a letter dated 9 January 1936, Fritsch wrote:

1) Any thoughts on the make-up and organization of tank units can be done only on a theoretical base, since we have no sufficient practical experience... The more we should observe the measures taken by those countries, which were not hampered by armament restrictions of the past fifteen years...

2) It is certain that in a coming conflict, our troops will have to fight with enemy tanks at any time... Our position is that all tanks will have to be armed with guns able to combat any enemy tank.

3) The 2cm MG [under development] can be reckoned as the lightest available anti-tank weapon. However, armour penetration data are

Kriegsgliederung d.1.Panzerdivision

The theoretical organizational structure of a *Panzerdivision* was elaborated on occasion of the establishment of the *Versuchs-Panzerdivision* in 1935. The chart shows the tank brigade with its two identical tank regiments. Each regiment had two battalions, made up of three light and one medium tank companies. The infantry brigade consisted of a rifle regiment and a motorcycle battalion. The divisional troops comprised an anti-tank battalion, a reconnaissance battalion, an artillery regiment, anti-aircraft, signals and pioneer elements. The chart does not show the supply services.

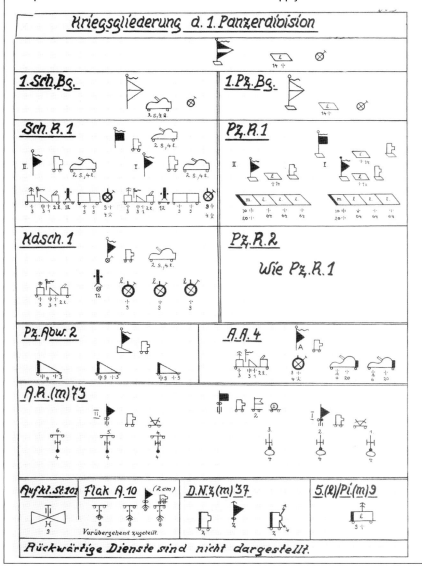

Above:
On the occasion of
Führergeburtstag
(Hitler's birthday), big
parades were conducted,
typical for dictators and
their obedient people.
Here PzKpfw I and II
turn into the West-Ost
Achse heading for the
Brandenburger Tor,
Berlin. Also only half a
year before the invasion
of Poland, no markings
are visible on the tanks.
(Author's collection)

considered as being insufficient. For this reason the bulk of our tanks should be armed with the 3.7cm TaK. The measures by foreign countries: namely France with the introduction of the 'Char D' clearly shows that emphasis is placed on a heavy gun armament. Despite this, it is beyond all doubt that tank units will need light tanks. The provision of an MG for these tanks used as reconnaissance vehicles may be sufficient, a 2cm MG is considered as the better solution.

4) As for organization and structure of tank units, GenStbdH defines its position as follows:

a) *Panzerregiment*:
The experiences of the next year will show whether the *Panzerzregimenter* will be provided with two or three *Panzer-Abteilungen* (battalions). GenStbH is sure that a structure of two *Abteilungen* per Regiment is the right decision. An independent *Panzerbrigade*, however, must command three *Abteilungen*. The brigade and battalion staffs must be provided with a reconnaissance platoon of five light tanks each.

b) *Panzerabteilung*:
We agree to the suggested structure:

- Staff with a signal and reconnaissance platoon
- Three light Pz *Kompanien*
- One heavy Pz *Kompanie*

c) *Panzerkompanie*:
… In GenStdH judgement the following structure of the light company (le Kp
– *leichte Kompanie*) is practical:

Company leader's vehicle	One Pz (3.7cm)
One reconnaissance platoon	Five Pz (MG or 2cm)
Three platoons with five Pz armed with 3.7cm TaK	15 tanks
	21 tanks

Furthermore we consider up to five tanks as reserve per company is desirable. Alternative a staff company according to the French example comprising of workshop platoon, replacement platoon and supply platoon is desirable.

The heavy company (s Kp – *schwere Kompanie*) will be held back to the disposal of the battalion leader (*Abteilungs-Führer*). This company does not need a reconnaissance platoon. The proposed structure:

Below:
A PzKpfw II stands on guard at an Austrian border post, the swastika flag erected. The *Anschluss* (union) with the *Reich* on 14 March 1938 was supported by the majority of Austrian citizens; those dissenting voices were prosecuted by the new leadership. (Baschin)

Company leader's vehicle	One Pz (7.5cm)
Four platoons with three Pz armed with 7.5cm gun	12 tanks
	13 tanks

5) ... The tank programme has to be adjusted to these proposals. According
   to these demands we will need 855 MG-armed tanks as reconnaissance
   vehicles...
   We urgently call on industry, which must increase the manufacture and
   delivery of heavy tanks. Firstly, all production of those tanks armed with
   3.7cm TaK must be accelerated.
   Any other equipment, even with 2cm-armed tanks, must be regarded as
   stop gap solutions...

In 1937, a training manual for the leichte Panzerkompanie was published.
Excerpt:

1) Organization and introduction
   In the year of training 1938 the complement of the light tank company will
   presumably reach the following status:
   HQ section: Two Pz 1, One Pz II, One kl PzBefWg (command tank)
   1.- 3. Platoon: Four Pz I, One Pz II
   4. Platoon: Five Pz II
   Total: 14 Pz I, Nine Pz II, One kl PzBefWg

This company brings the following weapons into combat:
    38 machine guns, in detail
    28 7.92mm MG 13K
    Ten 7.92mm MG 34
    Nine 2cm KwK 30…

In 1939, the last organizational structures before the beginning of the war were published. It should be made clear that these were the ideal and only valid on paper. Due to the shortages of 3.7cm armed tanks, at that time, many respective established posts had to be occupied with 2cm armed tanks, or PzKpfw II. However, the target figures for *Panzerbefehlswagen* (PzBefWg – armoured command tanks) were nearly achieved. The same was for the 7.5cm-armed tanks, called BW or PzKpfw IV.

Establishment of the first *Panzerdivisionen*

According to the above structure diagrams, by 1939 seven full-scale tank divisions had been established, each having one tank brigade with two tank regiments. Two battalions were issued to a regiment.

1. *Panzerdivision*
2. *Panzerdivision*
3. *Panzerdivision*
4. *Panzerdivision*
5. *Panzerdivision*
10. *Panzerdivision*
Panzerdivision Kempf (named after the commander).

Below:
A PzKpfw I Ausf B alongside a k PzBefWg command tank in a concealed position. The tactical symbol identifies both tanks as being from PzRgt 4. (NARA)

Above:
A platoon of LaS proceeds along a dirt track. Continuous manoeuvres not only helped to improve tactical methods but also identified any mechanical and technical problems with the design of the tanks. (NARA)

Right:
During transport on an *Autobahn* (motorway), this Büssing-NAG Typ 900 heavy truck has had to make an emergency stop. As a consequence the load, a PzKpw II Ausf C, has slid forward and demolished the driver's cab. (Hoppe)

The *leichte Division*

The years before outbreak of the war were used to establish Guderian's ideas of highly-mobile tank divisions. However, there were plans being made to establish even more mobile tank formations. The GenStbH set up requirements in June 1936:

> After the establishment of a *leichte Divisionen* was contemplated, we will comment on the proposed organizational structure and technical structure:
>
> 1) The tasks given to a 'light Division' require the compliance with the following organizational and technical demands:
>
> a) The light Division has to be '*leicht zu führen*', [easy to lead]. We need a short and simple chain of command. The subunits have to be internally established with all the weapons they need in combat. Marching group, billeting group and combat group have to be integrated.
> b) '*leichte Beweglichkeit*' (great mobility and agility), has absolute priority. The bulk of the vehicles must be small and highly mobile. For instance, the infantry elements should be provided with a great number of smaller vehicles instead of the large infantry transport vehicles. All vehicles in the combat units have to be easy to conceal in the combat zone. The only exception from that rule are the tanks and artillery tractors…

Below:
The *leichte Divisionen* were provided with a transport regiment to allow the fast transport of their tanks over long distances. The Faun L 900 D 576 heavy truck is loaded with a PzKpfw II Ausf D and tows an SdAnh 115 trailer loaded with a PzKpfw I Ausf A. (Erdmann)

Stabskompanie einer Panzer-Abteilung

The staff company of a tank battalion shows (from left to right) the combat column, the AA platoon, the pioneer section, the reconnaissance section, a signal platoon and a light tank platoon, provided with five MG or 2cm armed tanks.

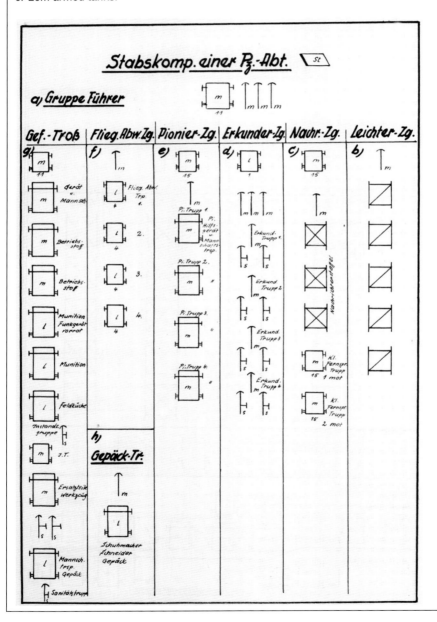

Leichte Panzer-Kompanie

The light company consisted of a light tank platoon issued with five 2cm-armed tanks, and three platoons with five 3.7cm armed tanks, at that time either PzKpfw III or Pzkpfw 35(t). The company headquarters section had two tanks.

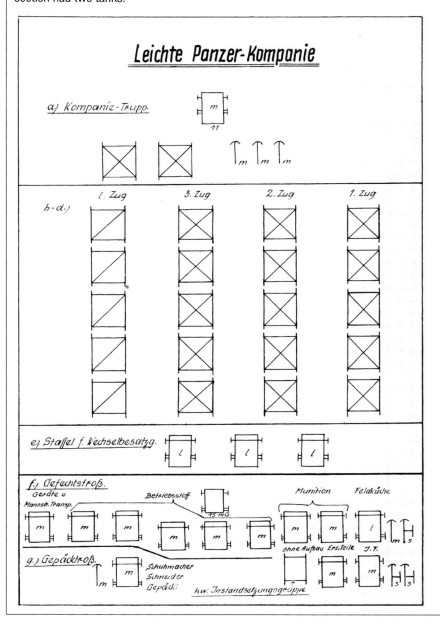

Mittlere Panzer-Kompanie

The heavy company of a tank battalion was issued with three platoons of four 7.5cm armed tanks (BW or PzKpfw IV) each. Two further PzKPfw IV were issued to the headquarters section. A light tank platoon, provided with five MG or 2cm armed tanks completed the company.

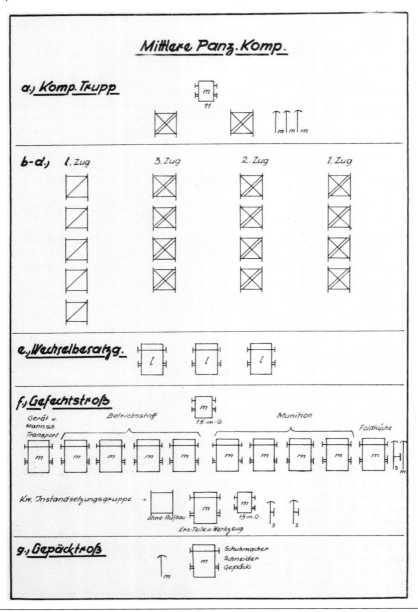

Additional notes:

1) The light Division will have only one tank battalion; the main strength of the unit will be armoured cars and infantry.
2) Thus the *leichte* Division will have two light rifle regiments with two battalions each…
3) A motor-cycle battalion will not be required.
4) There will be no machine-gun company, see 1a…

The report does not mention the most interesting feature of the proposed *leichte Divisionen* (leDiv). To ensure a maximum of strategic mobility, the units were subordinated with *Kraftwagen-Transportregimenter* (KwTrsptRgt) equipped with heavy trucks and flat-bed trailers which allowed the light Division to redeploy rapidly; if well-laid roads were at hand. This, however, would be a problem in eastern European countries where many roads had a soil (mud) or gravel covering.

Initially a specialized variant of the LaS 100 was developed for usage by the light Division. Later called PzKpfw II Ausf D, this tank was fitted with torsion-bar suspension as a solution to the increasing number of breakages of the leaf springs on earlier LaS vehicles. Thanks to an improved transmission, the Ausf D could attain very high road speed of over 55 kph. The proposed first production run of 85 vehicles was not reached due manufacturing problems. After 43 had been built, production of the PzKpfw II Ausf D halted.

Below:
Massed manoeuvres by the *Panzerwaffe* in PzKpfw I Ausf A were a common sight in the late 1930s. (Anderson)

Above:
The *Führer* takes the salute as three heavy trucks with trailers loaded with PzKpfw II Ausf D of a *leichte Division* parade past. Due to a lack of these fast tanks, four *leichte Divisionen* were issued with other versions of the PzKpfw II and some PzKpfw I. (Anderson)

It is possible that the decision to end production was made in conjunction with the decision to incorporate the *leichte Divisionen* into normal *Panzerdivisionen*. The *leichte Divisionen* were to be equipped with light tanks, possibly depending on availability.

However, by November 1938 four *leichte Divisionen* had been established: 1.leDiv (PzAbt 65), 2.leDiv (PzAbt 66), 3.leDiv (PzAbt 67) and 4.leDiv (PzAbt 33). Already under strength before the invasion of Poland: 1.leDiv underwent an extensive strengthening programme, the unit was reinforced by Pz Rgt. 11, converting it into a near standard *Panzerdivision*. The KwTrsptRgt was disbanded.

Establishment of independent tank brigades

Up to 1938, two independent *Panzerbrigaden* (4. and 6.PzBrig) were established. Organized at army troop level, the main task for these units was to clear the way for the advancing infantry divisions.

These brigades were disbanded until the war when they were quickly transferred to established incomplete tank divisions. 4.PzBrig was split; PzRgt.7 became part of *Panzerdivision* Kempf; PzRgt.8 became part of 10.PzDiv: six months later both were consolidated into 10.PzDiv. 6.PzBrig was also split, PzRg.11 became part of 1.leDiv. PzRgt. 25 remained as a reserve at army troop level.

Stabskomp einer R.Abt

This organizational structure shows one of the many concepts for a light Division. It comprises of three rifle battalions, one reconnaissance battalion and one motorized tank battalion. Of interest is the proposed *Stutmgeschütz-Abteilung* (1). The document notes that after allotment of the assault gun battalions, the anti-tank elements and one artillery battery were disbanded.

Vorschlag
für

Anlage zu 1.Abt.
Nr.922/36 g.Kdos.Ib

Kriegs Gliederung einer leichten Division.

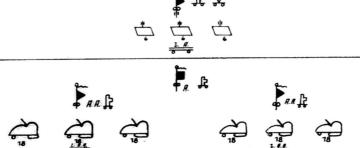

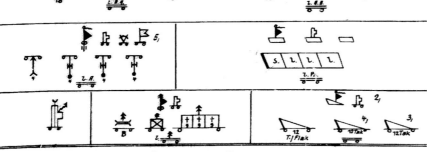

Rückwärtige Dienste:

Bemerkungen: 1) 1 Abt.Sturmartl. Falls Sturmartl.so konstruiert wird, dass sie Pz.Abwehr übernehmen kann, können 2)-4) fortfallen, andernfalls ist Verminderung von 5) um 1 Bttr.möglich.

CHAPTER 3

FROM THE LaS TO THE BW

The development of armoured fighting vehicles in Germany took many years. Between 1927 and 1932, only a few experimental tanks were designed and produced in different versions, the *Leichttraktor* and the *Grosstraktor*. However, both were of great importance for the German armaments industry. Despite being developed in strict secrecy, valuable experience was gained during this period. Experience with these first *Versuchsfahrzeuge* allowed important decisions to be made, which set the requirements for the coming *Panzerwaffe*:

- Light tanks armed with MGs or a 2cm gun
- Tanks armed with a 3.7cm armour-piercing gun
- Tanks armed with 7.5cm dual purpose gun

Interesting enough, in the early 1930s a further multi-purpose tank had been discussed:

- A tank armed with a 10.5cm tank. This vehicle was referred to as the Nebeltank and would assist their own units by setting a smoke screen in front of attacking enemy tanks. Furthermore effective high-explosive rounds should provide active fire support.

Neubaufahrzeug

The *Neubaufahrzeug* (NbFz) was developed and produced between 1933 and 1935. Following the style of the time, the tank was fitted with a main

Left:
The first production model of the 3.7cm KwK L/45 armed *Zugführerwagen* (ZW), was later designated as the PzKpfw III Ausf A. The vehicle had five large road wheels damped by externally mounted coils springs. Only ten were built, and all had been delivered by 1937. At that time a simple, but effective, numbering system was introduced; note the three-digit vehicle number stencilled on the rear of the turret. (Münch)

Above:
One of the Rheinmetall *Leichttraktoren*, the predecessor of the later PzKpfw III, was converted to a coil-spring suspension. (Münch)

Right:
Command tanks were an important factor in German military planning. The first *gepanzertes Führungsfahrzeug* was fabricated on the hull of the Krupp *Leichttraktor*. The large tube fitted on top of the vehicle was a telescopic radio mast. In the background are two of 20 LaS with superstructures and turrets fabricated from mild steel. (Hoppe)

turret and two auxiliary turrets. Mounting a 3.7cm armour-piercing gun and a 7.5cm heavy-support gun, the vehicle promised to be truly versatile, and was, together with the few *Leichttraktor* and *Grosstraktor*, thoroughly trialled in a number of smaller exercises and also in the great *Versuchsübung* (test manoeuvre) of 1935. The *Neubaufahrzeug* was the only design of the *Reichswehr* period to have a (theoretical) combat value. However, the NbFz proved to be impractical.

It is unnecessary to state that these existing designs were merely test vehicles not suitable to equip large tank formations. For a number of reasons it was important for the German authorities to establish these first tank units and supply them with large numbers of vehicles as rapidly as possible:

- The tanks were desperately needed for the practical training of the crews: the many thousands of *Panzermänner*.
- Tactical training within the tank units was considered to be of prime importance. The cooperation with infantry and support units required highly skilled officers, and the mutual understanding between the different forces.
- After having obtained the full military parity, Hitler was eager to build up the arms industry and build the skills to produce even more sophisticated weaponry, which he needed to back his aggressive foreign policy.
- The enormous armaments programme fell in a phase of economic recovery. Very much like the construction of the German *Autobahn* (motorway) network it certainly helped the regime to justify its claim to

Below:
The LaS 100 mounting a 2cm automatic gun was designed to support the LaS. This prototype hull is undergoing trials crossing a very temporary-looking pioneer bridge. (Historyfacts)

Above:
Tanks of 1.PzDiv parade through the city of Erfurt, Thuringia. The column tanks are led by a *kleiner Panzerbefehlswagen* (PzBflWg – command tank) based on the LaS. (Erdmann)

leadership. Tanks, much more than other weapons, could help to create a national enthusiasm, which possibly could heal the still ruffled ego of many, many Germans.

For the *Heereswaffenamt*, the office which had to organize the rearmament, a small and inexpensive tank was the prime solution. By choosing a tankette type of vehicle, the task seemed to be totally feasible.

In 1931, a small tracked vehicle was acquired from Vickers Carden-Loyd. This un-armoured chassis had simple running gear with four running wheels mounted in pairs and hung on leaf-sprung bogies. The final-drive sprocket was mounted at the front. This was the true forebear of the first tank mass produced by Germany.

LaS

Krupp, a company with a long history of manufacturing artillery pieces, was commissioned to develop a prototype for the first operational German tank. Designed from the beginning as an open-topped vehicle, it was designated as the *Landwirtschaftlicher Schlepper*, (LaS – agricultural tractor). In 1933, the vehicle had been completed and was delivered for series of exhaustive trials.

A year later, an armoured superstructure and a small turret, mounting two MGs, was fitted and the vehicle was ready for production.

The mechanical layout of the LaS, which differed from earlier designs, became the standard pattern for all future German tanks: steering system the transmission and drive sprockets located at the front, the engine and cooling system at the rear. A Cardan-type shaft transferred the power to the

Type Technical Data	Krupp *Leichttraktor*	Daimler-Benz *Grosstraktor*	*Neubaufahrzeug*
Armament	3.7cm 1 MG	7.5cm 3 MG	7.5cm 3.7cm 3 MG
Crew	Four	Six	Six
Radio	yes	yes	yes
Armour, frontal	14mm	14mm	16 - 20mm
Weight	8.7t	16t	23t
Performance	100hp	260hp	290hp
Max speed	30kph	40kph	30kph
Power/weight ratio	11.5hp/t	16.2hp/t	12.6hp/t
Ground pressure	0.73kg/cm²	0.53kg/cm²	0.69kg/cm²
Endurance	130km	150km	120km

Above:
A PzKpfw II on training exercise attempting to break through 'Hedgehog'-type concrete anti-tank and barbed-wire defences. When German forces invaded Greece this type of obstacle was found on the formidable Metaxas Line. (Anderson)

Type Technical Data	PzKpfw I Ausf A	PzKpfw I Ausf B
Armament	2 MG 34	2 MG 34
Crew	Two	Two
Radio	yes	yes
Armour, frontal	13 – 15mm	13 – 15mm
Weight	5.4t	5.8t
Performance	57hp	100hp
Max speed	37kph	42kph
Power/weight ratio	11.1hp/t	17.2hp/t
Ground pressure	0.39kg/cm²	0.52kg/cm²
Endurance	140km	170km

front. This gave the vehicle excellent weight distribution. The suspension consisted of a drive sprocket, four running wheels (mounted in pairs on leaf-sprung bogies) and a rear idler wheel. The linked tracks were supported by three return rollers.

The driver was seated in the left side of the superstructure. The fighting compartment was located in the centre of the chassis covered by a small turret, mounted slightly to the right. Due to it being relatively light, the turret was traversed manually. Two air-cooled, magazine fed Dreyse-type MG 13k (*kurz* – short) machine guns were mounted in the turret.

The 13mm steel armour protection was designed to withstand fire from 7.92mm armour-piercing ammunition. Each vehicle was equipped with a metric-wave radio receiver (*Ukw-Empfänger a*) installed in front of the commander. The radio and the weapons were operated by the commander.

By August 1935, 318 tanks had been delivered to the units. At around that time the official nomenclature was changed and the designation LaS was changed: the vehicle was now designated as the *Panzerkampfwagen* I (PzKpfw I). Some 1,300 vehicles had been delivered when production ceased.

Although the LaS were fitted with a radio receiver, company leaders reported the need for a radio transmitter. For this reason a *kleiner Panzerbefehlswagen* (kl PzBefWg – small command tank) equipped with a receiver and transmitter, was created by replacing the turret with a fixed

Below:
The PzKpfw I Ausf B had a lengthened hull and improved suspension to allow the installation of a more powerful and reliable Maybach NL 38TR engine developing 100hp. The first vehicles were delivered to tank units in early 1937. This vehicle was manufactured by Henschel (chassis No.12526). The checkerboard pattern around the top of the turret was used by 1.PzDiv. (Hoppe)

Above:
In 1936, production of the kl PzBefwg (SdKfz 265) was switched to the longer chassis of the PzKpfw I Ausf B, which gave more space to fit radio equipment and also a 7.92mm MG 34 machine gun. Later versions were fitted with an observation turret for the commander (Wilhelm)

housing. This enabled the company commander to communicate at command level of the *Abteilung*, and also to the tanks of his company.

The LaS was powered by an air-cooled Krupp M 305 engine delivering 57hp. Engine performance was soon regarded as being insufficient and the six-cylinder Maybach NL 38TR delivering 100hp was ordered as a replacement. To install this engine in the LaS, or PzKpfw I, the hull had to be heavily modified and this resulted in an increase of length by 40cm requiring the addition of a fifth running wheel. Subsequently, the original LaS was officially re-designated PzKpfw I Ausf A, the Maybach-engined vehicles as Ausf B. Approximately, 400 PzKPfw I Ausf B were built. A further 160 kl PzBefWg based on this vehicle were produced.

A significant number of open-topped *Fahrgestell für Schulfahrzeug* (training vehicles) were built using the chassis of both versions of the PzKpfw I.

Waiting for *schwere* Panzer

By the time the LaS was ready to enter production, German authorities had to learn that a considerable length of time was required to develop a tank before it was ready for production. Even when a tank was considered ready for production, it was not necessarily ready for combat. In April 1934, WaPrüf 6 delivered in an explanatory letter:

> The *Heereswaffenamt* oversees the production of prototypes built by many well-known companies (MAN, Daimler; Rheinmetall, Krupp, Henschel). It is essential that all of these *Versuchsfahrzeuge* [prototypes] will be thoroughly tested over a longer period. Furthermore, it is absolutely necessary to detect and revise any weaknesses in the design by exposing it to test firing and detonations. All this takes time… Failures occur, and detecting the problem is an arduous matter… Based on experiences with the MG-*Panzerkampfwagen*, any conversion to series production will certainly bring great problems… Therefore all schedules … can be given only under the stated prior conditions…

These few lines help to understand the discrepancies between the planned target figures given in 1936 (see Chapter 1) and reality. The report continues:

> The first prerequisite is to create a reliable design. If the schedule for series production is rushed, corrections in the series production are unpreventable and expensive, if possible at all. The combat value of

Below:
The first production model of the LaS 100, or PzKpfw II was the Ausf B, and a total of 100 were built. It was armed with a 2cm KwK 30 or 38 and a 7.92mm MG 34 in a co-axial mounting. The hull and superstructure had armour protection up to 14.5mm (Anderson)

Above:
A platoon of LaS on the training ground: The two leading tanks carry the skull on crossed bones pennant of the *Panzerwaffe*. It is possible that these tanks are painted in the soft-edged *Buntfarbenanstrich* (polychromatic finish) camouflage of the *Reichswehr*. (Anderson)

Type Technical Data	PzKpfw II Ausf c	PzKpfw II Ausf D
Armament	2cm KwK 1 MG	2cm KwK 1 MG
Crew	Three	Three
Radio	yes	yes
Armour, frontal	14.5mm	30mm
Weight	8.9t	11t
Engine power	140hp	140hp
Max speed	39.5kph	55kph
Power/weight ratio	15.7hp/t	12.8hp/t
Ground pressure	0.73kg/cm²	0.80kg/cm²
Endurance	190km	200km

tanks can be reduced to zero… It is necessary that the currently available production engineers, master craftsmen and skilled workers remain occupied. This requires that the MG PzKpfw and the 2cm MG PzKpfw remain in production until the heavier Panzer enters production. If a gap of several months occurs, the same problems will arise at the beginning of series production of the heavy tank as it happened in autumn 1934 during production of the MG PzKpfw

LaS 100 – a temporary solution

At the time the LaS was developed, its main armament was two 7.92mm MG 13k firing steel-cored ammunition which allowed the possibility of a defeating an enemy tank (at the time the majority of tanks had very light armour). A 2cm machine gun, with improved armour penetration, was being developed for the LaS. But for numerous reasons the idea of mounting this on the LaS chassis was soon abandoned.

Above:
A PzKpfw II Ausf B crashes through a brick-built obstacle during a training exercise. (Hoppe)

In 1934, WaPrüf 6 prescribed a development order for a tank in the 6-ton class. The project was designated LaS 100 (agricultural tractor, 100hp). A key feature was the armament, a 7.92mm MG 34: the new standard machine gun. Three companies, Krupp, MAN and Henschel were given development orders, but the MAN design was chosen.

Production began in October 1936. The tank followed the general construction of the LaS and was fitted with the Maybach NL38TR engine. The running gear consisted of six small running wheels, which were mounted in pairs on bogies similar to the LaS. The three bogies were stabilized by an externally-mounted long horizontal support.

The maximum thickness for the armour was still 13mm. Despite this thin armour protection, the LaS 100s was expected to perform a range of task including combat against enemy tanks. For this role it mounted a 2cm KwK 30 and an MG 34 in the turret. The gun was powerful enough to defeat a similarly armoured enemy tank at a range of around 500m.

It was originally planned that production should not exceed 200 tanks, but due to the delay in the development of the heavier tanks, it was decided to keep it in production. The first production types were the Ausf A, and Ausf B and a total of 175 were produced: Externally both very similar and only differed in small detail. The vehicle carried a crew of three, a commander, a radio operator and a driver.

The basic design was heavily modified and a second series, the Ausf C, entered production. A re-designed running gear with five larger running wheels mounted on cranks sprung by large leaf springs was fitted. Armoured protection was slightly increased to 14.5mm (this had begun on the Ausf B), and the power output of the Maybach engine was increased to 140hp.

A relatively small number of PzKpfw II Ausf C were built (75) from scratch. However, the PzKpfw II Ausf A to C, of which nearly 1,000 units were built, was basically identical to the Ausf c. The problem of identifying the types is made more difficult (sometimes impossible) by the fact that during their service life many exterior details such as extra armour and a cupola were retro-fitted.

The basic design of the MAN built PzKpfw II was not without problems. Although it would not be tested under fire for some years, day-to-day service in the *Panzerdivisionen* revealed many mechanical problems. In February 1937, the armaments manufacturer Alfried Krupp (AK), whose LaS 100 prototype was not chosen for production, made destructive comments on the PzKpfw II Ausf C currently manufactured by MAN:

Below:
A *Panzermann* in front of a PzKpfw I Ausf B probably in service with I./PzRgt 2. The vehicle carries and a three-digit (241) tactical number. Dust covers have been fitted over the armament. (Hoppe)

Left:
The *Battaillonsführer-wagen* (BW) or PzKpfw IV was introduced as a support vehicle armed with a 7.5cm KwK multi-purpose gun. The crews of these PzKpfw IV Ausf B or C tanks are using fire hoses to clean the mud off after a hard day on the training grounds. (Wilhelm)

Above:
The PzKpfw II Ausf C was fitted with simplified running gear consisting of five larger road wheels suspended on leaf springs. (Münch)

The small diameter road wheels wear out too quickly… The life span of the leaf springs… is only 1,500 to 2,500km…
… Access to the engine is poor because its location to the side. On average eight out of ten tanks issued to the troops are in the workshops for repair…
… Because of our greater experience, the LaS 100 built by AK is still completely operational today.

MAN knew about these problems. In 1937, the company proposed a re-design of their LaS 100. The engine and transmission were to be moved to the middle of the chassis, and to avoid the problems with the short service life the leaf springs, a new torsion-bar suspension was to be fitted. A more powerful Maybach HL 62TRM driving an SSG 46 gearbox was fitted, which allowed the maximum speed to be increased to 55kph. A unique detail on this vehicle was that it could be fitted with the same lubricated, rubber-padded tracks as being used by German half-track vehicles.

During the same period, the concept of the *schnelle* or *leichte Divisionen* was being discussed. The MAN design, sometimes referred to as the 'Schnellkampfwagen' (express tank), appeared to be the ideal vehicle. This was possibly the reason for the production approval of the new design and it entered (limited) production. It was designated the PzKpfw II Ausf D, and some 40 were built and issued to PzAbt (verl) 66 and 67.

ZW — the battle tank

In 1930, the German military, and nationalistic politicians like Hitler and his cohorts, saw their prime opponent in the west was France, their 'hereditary', or arch enemy. After the post-war experiences and the occupation of the Saar region by French troops, the German public was susceptible to such propaganda.

The German Intelligence service closely observed the technical and military developments throughout Europe, and especially in France. In his speech made during the great exercise of 1935, the commander-in-chief of the army emphasized:

> We have received information that France will develop and introduce some 1,000 tanks with increased armour protection of 40mm. Under this threat an offensive anti-tank defence has to be striven for...

This information was indeed true, as at that time the Renault R35 was in the process of being delivered to tank units. This threat called for vehicles with better armament and armour. Among the German military planners there was still some who believed that a machine-gun tank could, with certain limits, defeat an armoured opponent when using 7.92mm armour-piercing rounds. It became obvious to the German military that the LaS and

Below:
A PzKpfw II Ausf C has become bogged down during a training exercise over to marshy terrain and the crew is preparing to attach towing cable. The large numbers (409) stenciled white on the turret sides, do not match those (122) on the rhomboid plate. (Hoppe)

Above:
The PzKpfw III Ausf A was fitted with five large diameter running wheels and a distinctive 'low-slung' appearance. The frame positioned under the gun to push aside the radio aerial antenna when the turret was turned. Note the tank carries the solid cross used during the Polish campaign. (Anderson)

Type Technical Data	PzKpfw III Ausf A	PzKpfw IV Ausf A
Armament	3.7cm KwK 3 MG	7.5cm KwK L/24 2 MG
Crew	Five	Five
Radio	yes	yes
Armour, frontal	14.5mm	14.5mm
Weight	15t	18t
Performance	230hp	250hp
Max speed	35kph	33kph
Power/weight ratio	16.7hp/t	12.8hp/t
Ground pressure	0.68kg/cm²	0.68kg/cm²
Endurance	165km	210km

the LaS 100 (which had yet to enter production), could not defeat the armour of an R35.

A new tank designated *Zugführerwagen* (ZW – platoon leader's vehicle) was specified and the design of the type began with some urgency. At the end of 1934, Daimler Benz was contracted to develop a V*ersuchsfahrgestell* (test chassis) but the exact configuration of the suspension was still undecided. The ZW was proposed to be a 10 to 12-ton class tank, but the actual production version weighed 15 tons.

Krupp fabricated the turret which mounted a 3.7cm KwK L/46.5 and two MG 34 machine guns.

By February 1936, the *Oberkommando des Heeres* (ObdH – commander-in-chief of the army) announced during a conference with the war department heads:

1) ObdH agrees with the demand that the bulk of tank units shall be provided with an armour-piercing weapon of sufficient performance (3.7cm). Director WaPrüf.6 declares that the 3.7cm TaK can fight any modern tank… Development of 5cm and 7.5cm guns is on the way…
The proportion of MG-armed tanks and tanks fitted with an armour-piercing gun will depend on further experience gained in the near future. The idea to provide our units with tanks armed with armour-piercing guns in sufficient numbers to enable them to fight against enemy tanks; is totally correct…

Above:
TThe PzKpfw III Ausf B was fitted with improved suspension which consisted of eight small diameter running wheels mounted in pairs on small bogies; similar to the BW/PzKpfw IV. (Anderson)

Geheime Kommandosache

Anlage zu Nr. 2393 /37 g.Kdos. AHA Ib
vom 30. 10. 37

153

N a c h w e i s u n g

über den Rüstungsstand des Mob.Heeres nach dem Stande v.1.10.37

Stoff-glied. Ziff.	Benennung des Geräts pp.	1.Ausstattung (einschl. Ersatzheer)	monatlicher Nach-schub – Bedarf	Jst-Bestand am 1.10.37
1	Gewehre u.Kar.	1.532.727	85.120	1.363.075
2	M.G. (l.u.s.)	69.538	5.267	50.071
3	l.J.G.18	2.040	169	1.888
3	m.M.W.16	42	–	124
5	2 cm Kw.K.30	1.372	88	468
5	2 cm Flak 30	144	11	67
5	3,7 cm Pak	6.958	586	6.698
5	l.F.H.(16 u.18) (F.K.16 n/A.)	2.927	229	3.301
5	s.F.H.(13 u.18)	893	66	1.053
5	10 cm K.(17 u.18)	450	33	573
5	15 cm K.16	27	2	28
5	lg.21 cm Mrs.	23	2	28
13	Mun.für Gew.u.M.G.	314.159.370	314.159.370	3.833.356.000
13	" " l.J.G.18	306.000	306.000	2.451.400
13	" " m.M.W.16	1.550	1.550	8.465
13	" " 2 cm Gesch.	732.000	732.000	2.176.400
13	" " 3,7 cm	1.348.480	1.348.480	9.952.000
13	" " l.F.H.	522.000	522.000 (…) 7.020.400	
13	" " s.F.H.	99.600	99.600	1.294.600
13	" " 10 cm K.	49.800	49.800	728.750
13	" " 15 cm K.	2.640	2.640	33.536
13	" " lg.21 cm Mrs.	1.725	1.725	16.530
21	l.Panz.Spähwagen(Sd.Kfz. 221, 222 u.223)	571	51	511
21	s.Panz.Spähwagen(Sd.Kfz. 231, 232, 623 u. 624)	170	13	134
21	Pz.Kpf.Wagen I	1.835	113	1.468
21	Pz.Kpf.Wagen II	1.045	64	238
21	Pz.Kpf.Wagen III	70	6	12
21	Pz.Kpf.Wagen IV	61	5	–
21	Pz.Bef.Wagen	45	5	–
21	kl.Pz.Bef.Wagen	210	16	163

A document stamped 'Secret' detailing the planned and actual strength of the Panzerwaffe in 1937. (Anderson)

From a costs point of view, the decision to introduce the 3.7cm TaK for the proposed tank units is understandable. However, an early decision to develop a 5cm high-velocity gun would have given the *Panzerwaffe* a precious lead. However, it must be noted that in 1936, the 5cm gun was still being developed when the decision had to be made. However, the 3.7cm TaK was available.

The first chassis was fitted with five large-diameter running wheels mounted at cranks sprung by coil springs: a system which had been successfully tested on the *Leichttraktor*. The mechanical and interior layout was identical to all light tanks in German service, and the armour on the vehicle remained at 14.5mm. A more powerful Maybach HL 108TR engine, which developed 230hp, driving a ZF five-speed gearbox was installed. This first production vehicle was designated Ausf A.

The crew was increased to five: the commander sat in the turret, having an excellent view from his cupola. The gunner and loader were also positioned in the turret, to operate the main and machine-gun armament.

Above:
A total of 30 command tanks were built using the PzKpfw III Ausf D1 chassis. All German PzBefWg were available in two versions: the SdKfz 267 was used for contact between the companies and the battalion staff section and the SdKfz 268 for ground-to-air liaison. Externally there was no difference, but types were fitted with different radio equipment. (Anderson)

Above:
A PzKpfw IV Ausf D was powerful enough to plough through a pine forest, but the 7.5cm KwK would be seriously damaged if it were to strike a tree. (Anderson)

The driver sat in the left side of the hull, and the radio operator sat to the right. All modern German tanks were equipped with the *Funksprechgerät* 5 (Fu 5) transmitter and receiver and a *Funksprechgerät* 2 (Fu 2) receiver only radio.

A most significant feature introduced on the ZW (PzKpfw III), was the provision of an escape hatch for every member of the crew. A hatch (the commander had the cupola hatch) was installed in each side of the turret. The driver and radio operator were to use the maintenance hatches over the transmission.

In a report dated January 1936, the AHA (army office) reported:

Panzer units

1) AHA considers that the 3.7cm *Geschütz*-PzKpfw will not reach the necessary production efficiency to allow 100 tanks per month to be produced by 1 January 1938.
Reason: At present the first two *Versuchstücke* for the 3.7cm GeschPzKpfw are under trial. In technical respect, these two trial vehicles do not represent a base to permit mass production. In 1 April 1937, twenty-five 3.7cm GeschPzKpfw will be issued to the troop. These will be the vehicles of an O-series, or better *Versuchsserie*... Shortcomings and deficiencies of this trial series will have to be recognized and remedied, before mass production can start... Thus production cannot start before 1938; the first series production vehicles could reach the troop before autumn 1938. AHA is sure that this appreciation of the factual situation is an optimistic one.
2) For the 7.5cm GeschPzKpfw [see below, author] this statement is valid with a delay of six months...

While the Ausf A was in production, trials continued to improve the running gear. The next versions Ausf B, C and D were fitted with eight small diameter road wheels, mounted in pairs on swing axles fitted leaf-spring suspension.

The Ausf D served as a base for a larger *Panzerbefehlswagen* (large command tank), of which 30 were built. These specialized vehicles were issued to the staffs and headquarters of battalions, regiments and brigades. All were equipped with extensive radio equipment which had a range of up to 20km and allowed communication (by morse-code) with higher-command echelons. When equipped with *Fliegerfunkgeräte*, they served as ground-to-air liaison vehicles.

The ZW vehicles from the first production batches were issued to regular tank units, as the 3.7cm *Kampfwagen*. However, their entry into service was used as a continuation of the field trials, and during this period many design faults and weak components, especially in the suspension system, were found. This process continued throughout the production and service life of the Ausf A to D.

After the type had been first deployed in combat, all early versions were passed to *Panzer-Ersatz und Ausbildungsabteilungen* (training units) in 1940.

When the Ausf E (5/ZW) entered mass production all the major changes were introduced: in fact the vehicle was virtually completely redesigned. The maximum frontal armour was increased to 30mm, making the PzKpfw III Ausf E the best protected German tank at that time. The suspension was replaced with a torsion-bar system with six road wheels: a very significant decision. The vehicle was fitted with a more powerful Maybach HL 120TRM engine, which produced 320hp and drove a ZF Variorex 76 ten-speed semi-automatic gearbox. This enabled the tank to travel at over 60kph, but this high speed reduced the running life of the road wheels – and also the gearbox.

The re-design of these and other components was to cause serious delays in the production of the vehicles.

Deliveries began in 1938, and 96 PzKpfw III Ausf E and also 45 PzBefWg Ausf E (command tanks) were produced and issued to the troops. At the end of this production batch, further *Ausführungen* (F to N) followed and each incorporated improvements gained from experience in front-line service.

BW – the support tank

With development and production of the few *Neubaufahrzeuge*, an interesting line of technical development was started. However, the trials ended when the tank was withdrawn from service, but a few were used in Norway.

However, the requirement for a 7.5cm gun tank having been set, the HWa requested a replacement and both Rheinmetall and Krupp showed an interest in obtaining the development and production order. This proposed tank would (including the heavier ammunition) have a combat weight of 18 tons.

Below:
The short-barreled 7.5cm *Kampfwagenkanone* (KwK) L/24 was the standard main gun on the PzKpfw IV. At that time the tank entered service, the length of the gun barrel was considered to be important, as there were fears that a long gun would be too cumbersome when traversing the turret. Shown is a PzKpfw IV Ausf B which had armour of 30mm thick, almost twice the thickness on the Ausf A. (Historyfacts)

In March 1936, the ordnance office wrote a report dealing with the future development of the *Panzerwaffe*.

Development of PzKpfw…

The principal tasks of the *Panzerwaffe* can be summarized as:

a) Assistance of the infantry attack
b) Anti-tank defence
c) Independent operational combat in cooperation with other motorized forces… Based on these tasks weight limits of 8t to 18t were defined for the available tanks, and those being under development (MG, 2cm, 3.7cm and 7.5cm PzKpfw). Having these limits in mind, their tactical capabilities were focused on high engine output to reach high average top speed, agility and mobility… We therefore demand that a great part of those PzKpfw being issued to support the infantry have to be sufficiently armoured against the French 25mm Hotchkiss automatic gun. Regarding the tanks already issued and those to be developed (MG, 2cm, 3.7cm and 7.5cm) importance is attached to the armour protection:

Above:
The fourth production batch of the BW was the Ausf D, now had 30mm face-hardened frontal armour which offered full protection against 20mm anti-tank fire. Unlike the PzKPfw III, the PzKpfw IV had two escape hatches positioned in front of the turret for the driver and radio operator. (Anderson)

MG, 2cm and 7.5cm PzKpfw have to be safe against AP rounds fired from infantry weapons at all ranges.
The 3.7cm PzKpfw has to be safe against frontal fire from the 25mm Hotchkiss automatic gun...

Regarding the effect of our own weapons, the suitability of the following types for supporting the infantry is as follows:

a) The MG PzKpfw with two MG (MG 13k)
Judged by the effect of its weapons, the MG PzKpfw is well suited, the disadvantages of its weak armour (only SmK safe) will be neutralized by the small silhouette and its lower unit price (mass production)

b) The 2cm MG PzKpfw with one MG (MG 34)
Offers an MG 34 with high rate of fire and an AP gun. It is manoeuvrable and costs only some 50 percent of the 3.7cm gun tank.

c) The 3.7cm PzKpfw with three MG 34

The effect of its weapons (one 3.7cm, three MG) is favourable. Its armour protection is superior to all other (German) tanks

d) The 7.5cm PzKpfw with two MG 34

The power of its weapon is effective especially against the heavy weapons of enemy infantry and against anti-tank guns. Due to its weak armour it can be used only in the second wave of the tank attack...

The report ends:

Conclusion

The present German lines of development resulted in tanks suited for operative applications rather than for supporting the infantry assault. In respect of the weight limitation of 18t, the armour protection was deliberately held at a modest level. However, the development of the anti-tank weapon is

Above:
Poland 1939: Two PzKpfw I Ausf B of the *leichter Panzerzug* (light tank platoon) of an unknown *Panzerabteilung* advance across an open area to attack enemy infantry positions. The lead vehicle carries the solid-type cross only used for this campaign. (Prigent)

alarming. … All four tank types are not in danger from fire from machine guns. AP infantry rounds, however, can be fatal for most German designs. 2cm and 2.5cm weapons will penetrate the armour of the MG, the 2cm, the 7.5cm PzKpfw and, to some extent, the frontal armour of the 3.7cm PzKpfw. Considering this, a review of the armour question is inevitable…

These words show that Guderian's idea of committing tanks as the spearhead for breakthrough missions were generally accepted: the high speed of the tank allowed targets to be easily achieved. However, speed was influenced by the weight of the vehicle which affected the desired power to weight ratio: any improvements in armour protection would downgrade this ratio. However, the frontal armour on all German tanks (except the LaS) was increased, some before the outbreak of the war, others at the beginning of 1940. The weight limit was forgotten.

A successor for the *Neubaufahrzeug*

In 1934, the successor to the *Neubaufahrzeug* was developed under the code name BW (Begleitwagen – escort tank).

The basic design for the first *Versuchsstücke* was similar to that of the ZW, and the layout of the drive train was almost identical. Like Daimler-Benz, Krupp developed two different types of running gear. One had eight road wheels, mounted in pairs on a leaf-sprung bogie; the other had six road wheels and torsion-bar suspension. However, Krupp experienced severe technical problems with the sophisticated torsion-bar system, and as a consequence the BW was fitted with eight road-wheel suspension. Krupp would never use the torsion-bar system again.

Below:
The first production version of the PzKpfw IV, the Ausf A, had a rounded lower edge to the bow (glacis) plate, and (compared to later versions) wider superstructure. A simple cylindrical-shaped commander's cupola was fitted on the top of the turret. The Ausf A had frontal armour which was only 14.5mm thick, but it had already been decided to improve this before the outbreak of the war. (Prigent)

The construction of hull and superstructure allowed two large access hatches to be fitted in front of the turret. Like the ZW, the vehicle carried a five-man crew. All BW tanks issued to a platoon or company leader were fitted with Fu 5 and Fu 2 radio equipment; standard tanks had a receiver only. There were no plans to produce a command tank.

A 7.5cm KwK L/24, which fired high-explosive (HE), armour-piercing (AP) rounds and smoke shells, was mounted in the turret. A co-axial MG 34 was mounted alongside the main gun for close defence. A ball-mounted MG 34 fitted in the front plate was fired by the radio operator.

The first version, the Ausf A, had armour with a maximum thickness of only 14.5mm, but this was soon deemed to be insufficient. After 35 vehicles had been delivered, production of the Ausf B and C began and a number of improvements were made. The hull had thicker (30mm) frontal armour and the turret was altered by fitting an improved commander's cupola which offer better protection.

Production of heavy German tanks started at a very slow pace. In October 1937, the inventory of the *Panzerwaffe* was as follows:

PzKpfw I	1468
PzKpfw II	238
PzKpfw III	12
PzKpfw IV	--

What a contrast to the target figures of 1936 (see page 123).

Above:
A PzKpfw IV crosses over an obstacle on the training grounds. Before World War II, great importance had been placed on the training of new tank crews; especially drivers. Later in the war, the quality of training significantly worsened due to the lack of training vehicles and the severe shortage of fuel. (Anderson)

CHAPTER 4

THE CONDOR LEGION

In some aspects, the situation in Spain represented the political division in Europe: the democratic states in the west, Germany and Italy ruled by national-fascists and a communist Soviet Union.

The League of Nations and the European nations pursued a policy of non-interference, while Germany and Italy decided to give direct support to the nationalist side in Spain. However, the Soviet Union backed the republican side and the previously insignificant communist movement.

In 1936, the conflict became an all-out war. The decision by the western nations not to support the republicans led both Stalin and Hitler to authorize the delivery of military equipment and personnel to their chosen sides in Spain. In the coming months the Soviet Union delivered aircraft and more than 600 T-26 and BT-5 light tanks. By the current standards this was a very strong force indeed.

At approximately the same time, Nazi Germany supported Franco´s nationalist troops also with deliveries of aircraft and tanks. In October 1936, Germany delivered approximately 100 PzKpfw I to Spain.

The General Maxime Weygand, a French senior officer was certainly not an enthusiast of modern mobile warfare. In a foreword to a book, written by General Raymond Duval in 1938, dealing with the Spanish Civil War he makes a subtle analysis of the facts:

At the beginning, the government possessed all instruments of power: an army and sufficient military equipment, by far the largest part of Spanish territory, the gold reserves, the harbours and the fleet... But this

Left:
The commander of a PzKpfw 1 Ausf A in service with Spanish Nationalist forces signals that the town of Borriol has been taken during the fighting in the Province of Castellón in mid-1938. (Getty)

Above:
The fast tank BT-5 was built using the suspension system developed by inventor J.W. Christie, the Soviet Union having obtained a licence in the early 1930s. The BT-5 was lightly armoured and mounted a 45mm gun powerful enough to fight any tank of its time. This BT-5 has been captured was abandoned by its Republican Army crew. (von Aufsess)

government was not master of itself, it was under influence of outside interests. It may have had passion, but no ideals. Furthermore it was not able to establish, organize and form an army; whatever it collected under its colours was a confused horde...

For example, both parties had certain numbers of weapons of modern and sophisticated designs available. The flying forces were mainly deployed against ground troops; there was no interception of bombers. Armoured vehicles were used frequently. However, when losing the support of the infantry, these were quickly defeated by enemy artillery. However, the (benefit of the) machine must not be considered without the men operating it and the tactical idea behind them... Since both sides did not possess sufficient numbers or artillery, the fighting was more or less reduced to infantry battles. Thus we are unable to gain experience for the deployment of those modern weapons in greater formations... However, engineers will

gain valuable experience about the quality or deficiencies of the tanks´ machinery, armament and armour.

General Raymond Duval gave an interesting resumé in his book:

The results of the war in Spain can only disappoint the protagonists of modern strategy and tactics… It is said that the war of tomorrow will be a war of total annihilation, sacrificing both armed forces and civilians. Its only tools will be squadrons of aircraft and mechanized tank units. Thus there are men advancing their views that no other weapons than aircraft and tanks will be necessary in the future. The most determined advocates of these ideas go so far to state that aircraft alone will be sufficient…
The war in Spain did not prove the proponents of these exaggerated thought… However, there is certainly no reason to say that air raids will be without effect or tanks might be helpless against anti-tank weapons…

Above:
A Spanish Nationalist trooper practices firing a *Maschinengewehr* (MG) 13k which was the MG used in the PzKpfw I. The magazine-fed gun could also be used as an infantry weapon. (NARA)

Type Technical Data	Light Tank PzKpfw I Ausf A	Light Tank T-26 M 1933
Armament	2 MG	45mm 1 MG
Crew	Two	Three
Radio	yes	only command vehicles
Armour, frontal	14.5mm	15mm
Weight	5.4t	9.6t
Engine Power	60hp	90hp
Max speed	37kph	32kph
Power/weight ratio	11.1 hp/t	9.4 hp/t
Ground pressure	0.39 kg/cm²	0.66 kg/cm²
Endurance	140km	140km

Below:
Spanish Nationalist forces often made use of captured enemy material, including tanks. The T-26 was fitted with the same turret and 45mm main armament as that on the BT-5. (Anderson)

Mechanized tank divisions played no role, because no side was able to establish such formations. This reason might sound ridiculous, but it has a deeper truth. War can be waged only with the material which is at hand. For this reason it seems to be clear that the first tank battles of a coming war will resemble the last manoeuvers in peacetime.

This last sentence indeed shows a deeper truth. The experiences in World War I were still alive, and it was both tempting and dangerous to transfer them to the reality of 1938. From 1914 to 1918, the military became more powerful as every month passed, and technical progress in the inter-war period led to a further increase. However, this massive military power was intended to be effective in both defence and attack. New approaches were necessary to prevent a repetition of the trench warfare in World War I.

Duval and many military leaders, including Fuller, De Gaulle and Guderian, were advocates of modern warfare, and the deployment of combined weapons. However, these ideas had to be practised, and in

Below:
The left track and the drive sprocket have been removed and the transmission cover opened on this PzKpfw I Ausf A. Due to the dark-coloured paint finish, the light tank was often called 'Negrillo' by the Nationalist forces. (Anderson)

Above:
A *Panzerbefehlswagen* I was a commander's variant of the PzKpfw I Ausf B. These early vehicles did not have a ball mounting for the machine gun due to a shortage of supply, requiring it to be mounted on a temporary bracket. (Anderson)

peacetime this was possible only on the training grounds. Quite understandably, this first armed conflict in Europe was thoroughly observed and evaluated by Germany and the Soviet Union, and also the western European countries. In February 1939, after three long years of bloody fighting, the war ended. The nationalist forces were victorious and their leader Franco took power and established a dictatorship.

Practical implications for the *Panzerwaffe*

The first contingent of the Condor Legion sent to Spain, included a small detachment of light tanks commanded by *Oberstleutnant* Ritter von Thoma. These, manned only by Spanish nationalists, were deployed in combat for the first time in early 1937. After the battle, von Thoma sent an after action report:

Above:
When compared to Soviet-built T-26 and BT-5 tanks, the PzKpfw I was seriously under-gunned. The penetration power of the SmK ammunition was effective only at very short ranges. For this reason an unknown number of PzKpfw I, delivered to the Spanish Nationalists, were modified by installing a Solothurn 20mm automatic gun in a larger turret. (Anderson)

Above:
The mounting of the Solothurn gun was expertly carried out as a field modification by German engineers. However, further information on this modification has not been found. (Anderson)

Combat experiences from the fighting between German MG-armed tanks and Soviet gun tanks:

The detachment of German tanks consisted of PzKpfw I and kl PzBefWg tanks… The Republican insurgents were equipped with light tanks armed with 4.5cm guns. From the beginning, as it was in World War I, it was clear that the gun tank is superior to the MG tank.

During the first days of combat our MG-tanks could compensate for this drawback by using special SMK munition (amour-piercing rounds). After their first tank losses the Repulicans quickly realized that these rounds could penetrate the Soviet tanks up to ranges of 120 to 150m only… The countermeasure against our tanks was simple and was used immediately: the Soviet tanks did not come within combat range. When they observed MG tanks, they remained at ranges of not less than 1,000m. They moved into position and opened accurate fire with their guns. Our special purpose ammunition was useless at these

Above:
A Soviet-supplied T-26 in service with Republican forces during the Spanish Civil War. (Getty)

ranges. Furthermore, targeted fire was difficult, because our tanks could not halt. If they stopped, they were hit by enemy gun fire. A number of tanks were lost and their crews killed.

For this reason we have an urgent demand for gun tanks. If by this time no tank gun has been developed, we urge the installation of the 2cm KwK from the armoured cars instead.

Indeed at least one PzKpfw I Ausf A was modified by mounting a Solothurn 2cm gun.

However, due to the fact that the Spanish crews were untrained, and their leaders could hardly be called skilled soldiers, the value of tanks in

Below:
After the conclusion of the Spanish Civil War, the German contingent was honoured at a parade in Berlin held on 6 June 1939. The placards carry the names of all the German soldiers who died in the conflict. (Anderson)

Spain was negligible. Guderian stated that tank deployment in Spain was on too smaller a scale to allow any accurate assessment militarily or strategically.

However to the General Staff of the Army, much valuable experience had been gained. The commitment of tanks in an armed conflict, even under very simple circumstances: and when manned by untrained personnel allowed a much more accurate evaluation of this mode of warfare than was possible in any peacetime manoeuvres.

To summarize, in a final report published shortly before outbreak of the war in 1939, it stated that the mechanical reliability of the tanks was surprisingly good.

Above:
A kl PzBefWg and a PzKpfw I Ausf A and in a Spanish town, both vehicles have Nationalist identification colours painted on the superstructure. Just visible in the background is a captured Soviet tank, the T-26 in particular was highly prized by German tank crews. (Anderson)

Left:
General von Thoma, commander of the Condor Legion, takes a report from *Leutnant* Hoffmann at a parade of German tank instructors at their base in Cubas de la Sagra, near Madrid. Panzer units sent to Spain were given the codename Group '*Drohne*'. (Getty)

CHAPTER 5

1938 – ANNEXATION OF CZECHOSLOVAKIA

More Panzer for the army

By mid-1930, large parts of the Czech population (an estimated 24 per cent), in particular the regions around the western cities of Eger and Aussig also Troppau, were German-speaking. The Czechoslovak Republic was established after the war in 1918, marking the final end of the multi-ethnic Austro-Hungarian Empire. This region was commonly known as Sudetenland, as it was divided by the Sudeten mountains.

A new state was proclaimed, an extensive level of independence was promised to all national minorities. However, this promise was never implemented and the German-speaking citizens felt suppressed, having failed to gain autonomy. In 1933, a national-socialist party became the most influential political power in the Sudetenland. Those in nationalist circles living in the Sudeten region proclaimed more or less open affiliation to the German *Reich* and, quite naturally, Hitler supported their efforts. When this matter turned into a crisis for Europe, all attempts at mediation by the western states failed. Following unachievable demands made by the Sudeten party; the Czechoslovak government declared a partial mobilization of its military which aggravated the crisis.

The *Anschluss*, the annexation of Austria to Germany in 1938, brought further troubles.

On 30 August 1938, the OKH reviewed the situation:

Left:
A PzKpfw II Ausf C of PzRgt 6 (3.PzDiv) parades through Prague on 17 March 1939. In the background is the Hotel Sroubek (now the Europa).

Above:
After the annexation, *Generaloberst* von Brauchitsch, the supreme commander of the army, visited Reichenberg (now Liberec) one of the German-speaking enclaves in the western part of the Czech Republic. His transport was a six-wheeled Mercedes G4 cross-country car, and was necessary due to the poor condition of (or lack of) paved roads. (NARA)

Continous draft calls for recruits and reserve soldiers… and a steady extension of fortifications confirm the reports that the Czechs are expecting a German invasion in the autumn of this year… The German manoeuvers and the establishment of German reserve units contribute to increase pressure on Czech… The morale of the Czech army is bad. While solely pure-bred Czech units (IR 46) are determined to offer stiff resistance, the situation in other units of mixed nationalities is unsettled (IR 6).

Both Britain and France were in favour of assigning the German-speaking regions to Germany, but insisted on international guarantees for the Czechoslovak Republic. Hitler who, from the beginning, intended to destroy the state. After further political unrest, the Czechs proclaimed total mobilization. At the infamous conference in Munich, held between 29 and 30 September 1938, Britain, France and Italy agreed to the Sudetenland being assigned to the German *Reich*. No representative of the Czechoslovak Republic was invited to attend the meeting.

In a situation review No. 49 from the OKH dated 1 October:

With approval of the conditions negotiated in Munich by Germany, Britain, France and Italy, no resistance of the Czech units stationed in the border regions is anticipated.

Having reached his first target, Hitler now decided to solve the matter by military means. On 1 October 1938, German troops marched into the region and the Czechoslovak state was dissolved in early 1939. Slovakia was to remain an autonomous state.

For Hitler this development was very favourable. The German economy received a boost due to the industrial strength of the annexed country, which had an established heavy industry which also manufactured armaments.

For Germany, this boost came at a decisive period. Almost immediately after the agreement made in Munich, all the Bohemian and Moravian steel and manufacturing industry acquiesced to German demands. The factories of all existing companies producing automobiles and tanks were inspected. Some companies, among them Českomoravská Kolben-Daněk (CKD), which became Bömisch Mährische Maschinenfabrik AG (BMM), and Škoda were producing high-quality armoured vehicles.

Below:
The Czech-built LT vz 35 was a 'modern' light tank armed with a 37mm main gun and built with frontal armour of 25mm. This tank is still painted in the original camouflage and carries a Czech army registration number. (Hoppe)

Left:
General Reinhardt takes the salute as a column of PzKpfw IV Ausf A German tanks parades through the town of Komotau on 9 September 1938. As was common practice the market place has already been renamed Adolf Hitler Platz. (NARA)

Škoda LT vz 35

In the early 1930, Škoda had begun the design and development of the *Lehký Tank vsor 35* (Light Tank, model 35) and by 1938 the vehicle was ready for production.

The light tank was fabricated from armoured-steel plates which were riveted together. Frontal armour was 25mm thick. The 8,600cc Škoda T 11/0 four-cylinder petrol engine was mounted in the rear of the hull, as were the gearbox and final drive. The driver was assisted by a sophisticated pneumatic steering, brake and clutch-operating system, which also saved precious space. The running gear was a modified version of the famous Vickers design. The main armament, a 37mm Škoda A7 gun, had a performance comparable with any contemporary tank gun. For self-defence, a 7.92mm ZB (machine gun) was installed in the turret and another in the hull.

Originally the LT vz.35 had a crew of three; a commander, who had to handle the main and secondary ordnance, a driver and a wireless operator, who also had to operate an the machine gun in the front plate.

The LT vz.35 was almost immediately adopted by the Germans, and the vehicle was fitted with a standard Fu 5 radio transmitter and receiver. The crew was increased to four by including a gunner.

In the time following the occupation approximately 200 of the type, (later designated PzKpfw 359(t) (*tschechisch* – Czechoslovak), were used to establish

Below:
After the occupation of the remaining parts of the Czech Republic, German forces immediately searched for and seized all military material. Here the hull of a prototype discovered at the Skoda works is about to be hauled away by an LT vz 35. (Anderson)

Type Technical Data	PzKpfw 35(t) LT Vz 35	PzKpfw 38(t) LT Vz 38
Armament	3.7cm L/40 2 MG	3.7cm L/48 2 MG
Crew	Three, in German service Four	Three, in German service Four
Radio	yes	yes
Armour, frontal	25mm	25mm
Weight	10.5t	9.7t
Engine power	120hp	125hp
Max speed	34kph	42kph
Power/weight ratio	11hp/t	12.8hp/t
Ground pressure	0.50kg/cm²	0.57kg/cm²
Cruising range, max	219km	250km

Below:
German tank crews testing the off-road performance of an un-armed LT vz 35 light tank. The riveted construction is clearly visible. (Baschin)

Above:
The Czech-built LT vz 38, came as an absolutely surprising for the German inspectors. Although of riveted construction, it proved to be a rugged and reliable, well-balanced tank and was used by the *Panzerwaffe* in significant numbers. (Historyfacts)

Above:
Although the suspension on a PzKpfw 38(t) resembled the Christie-type it was, however, conventionally sprung with leaf springs. (Anderson)

Left:
The PzKpfw 38(t) was armed with a 3.7cm Skoda A7 (KwK 38[t] L/47.8) main gun and two 7.92mm ZB-53 (MG 37[t]) machine guns. Originally the vehicle carried 90 rounds of 3.7cm ammunition, but this was reduced to 72 when the Germans added a loader to the crew. Also 2,550 rounds of 7.92mm machine gun ammunition were carried. (Anderson)

Above:
A pre-production TNHP-S at the Prague factory of Ceskomoravska Kolben Danek (Böhmisch-Märische Maschinenfabrik [AG] after 1940), and the type continued in production until 1942. The tank was also exported to Spain, Switzerland and Peru and many were built under licence. The vehicle was adopted by the *Panzerwaffe* as the PzKpfw 38(t). (Vaclev)

three German *Panzerabteilungen* (tank battalions) which were combined into the *1.leichte* Division. In this unit they were used in place of PzKpfw IIIs, which were not available in sufficient numbers. A number of these tanks were converted to *Panzerbefehlswagen* (command tank) with special radio equipment to allow contact with higher-command echelons.

CKD/BMM LT vz 38

During a visit to BMM, German inspectors were surprised to find a light tank which just completed the development programme.

The hull and superstructure of the LT vz 38, was also of riveted construction with 25mm (maximum) thick armour; this was almost comparable to that of the German PzKpfw III.

The running gear consisted of four large-diameter road wheels suspended on leaf springs, two return rollers and well-designed sturdy tracks. The vehicle followed 'standard' German tank-design practice: the 7,754cc Praga, (a licence-built Swedish Scania-Vabis 1664) six-cylinder engine was mounted in the rear compartment and attached by a Carden-type shaft to the transmission at the front of the vehicle. Due to the relatively low weight of the tank it proved to be very reliable. The main armament was upgraded and designated 37mm KwK 38(t) L/47.8 gun. As on the Lt vz 35(t), a 7.92mm ZB (now MG 37[t]) machine gun was mounted in the turret and another in the front plate.

As the production lines were ready, the German occupiers ordered production to commence. After a rapid evaluation programme a number modifications were incorporated (including provision for a fourth crew member [gunner]).

A total of 78 PzKpfw 38(t) were delivered to the *Panzertruppe* before 1939, the largest number being issued to 3.*leichte Division*.

In October 1938, the *Panzerwaffe* reported the following tank strength (left cplumn), the right column shows the respective target figures specification for 1936. Most certainly the figures were objectives only, and written with a certain degree of uncertainty. However, the extraordinary disparity regarding the more powerful types, the 3.7cm and 7.5cm armed tanks, clearly shows the uncertainty in the planning process, and also the problems within the German armaments industry:

PzKpfw I	1,468	825 = combined numbers of
PzKpfw II	823	PzKpfw I and PzKpfw II
PzKpfw III	59	1,885
PzKpfwg IV	76	468
kleiner PzBefWg	180	----
grosser PzBefWg	2	----

Below:
The Lt vz 38 in its original configuration. The tube mounted along the left-hand side is the aerial for the radio equipment. Although the vehicle appears ready for service Czech camouflage, the armoured guard for the driver's vision visor is missing. (Netik)

CHAPTER 6

FALL WEISS — THE INVASION OF POLAND

On 1 September 1939, the German war machine attacked the Republic of Poland after a perfectly orchestrated *Zwischenfall* (incident) at the German-Polish border. There was no official declaration of war, but nonetheless the German propaganda spoke of a forced, but inevitable war. Indeed, a document dated April 1939 declared:

SPECIAL REGULATIONS FOR *FALL WEISS*

Legal fundamentals:

We have to assume that no official declaration of war will be given… The Hague regulations will similarly apply …

Quite naturally, the complete campaign was thoroughly pre-planned as far back as the mid-1930s. Two *Heeresgruppen* (army groups) were formed, and further forces were positioned in East Prussia, the German province cut off by the Polish Corridor. *Heeresgruppe Nord* (Army Group North) was to advance, supported by these troops, to the line of the rivers Nogat, Vistula and Dwręca, establish bridgeheads and then the advance towards Warsaw would commence.

Heeresgruppe Süd (Army Group South) was ordered to march into Poland from the west and the south in order to take the Polish industrial region of Silesia. They were then to take up defensive positions on the bank of the river Warta in preparation for an expected counterattack by Polish forces coming from Upper Silesia.

Left:
The PzKpfw II was deployed in larger numbers than any other German tank during the invasion of Poland. Introduced only shortly before the invasion, a large white cross for identification has been painted on the mantlet. An early version of the Notek Nachtmarschgerät (night-driving device) is mounted in front of the turret, one of the many improvements fitted after delivery. (Anderson)

Right:
A later production kl PzBefWg, built on the PzKpfw I Ausf B chassis, but due to its box-like superstructure it was easily identifiable as a command tank to the enemy. Later PzBefWg which used the PzKpfw III chassis were externally almost identical to the combat tank. (Anderson)

Below:
Tanks of 4.PzDiv assemble in a shallow depression. The kl PzBefWg to the right is part of the staff section of I.*Abteilung* of either PzRgt 35 or 36. The PzKpfw II Ausf C in the foreground has the three-tailed star divisional emblem used only during this campaign. (Anderson)

Poland: strength of *Panzerwaffe* in 1939							
PzKpfw I	1,026	PzKpfw II	1,151	PzKpfw III	87	PzKpfw IV	197
PzKpfw 35(t)	164	PzKpfw 38(t)	57	PzBefWg	177	**Total:**	**2,859**

Starting position

By the summer of 1939, the German army had seven regular *Panzerdivisionen* operational; a further four *leichte Divisionen* provided fast-reacting attack forces. Two tank regiments formed an operational reserve at army troop level.

The German *Panzerwaffe* had a force of some 2,800 tanks available, but most of these were light tanks and of only limited combat value. However, all Polish tanks had only thin armour protection, which allowed even the machine-gun armed PzKpfw I to be used with some success when using armour-piercing ammunition.

The Polish army had a total of 400 tanks in service. Some 150 reasonably modern developments of the Vickers Mk E. Designated 7 TP, it was diesel-powered and built in two versions: the 7 TP DW with two separate machine-gun turrets, or (TP JW) mounting a 37mm Bofors gun in one large turret. In September 1939, most had been converted to the JW standard. These tanks were certainly superior to the German light tanks, and from a purely technical point of view should be capable of defeating all German types.

Below:
A PzKpfw II Ausf a1 negotiates a deep trench, as the commander carefully looks out of his hatch. The first 75 production vehicles were fitted with six small running wheels mounted on three bogies and supported by a metal beam. (Anderson)

Course of the Polish Campaign

The daily situation reports from the OKH give a good idea of the German assault:

> The deployment of the German forces proceeded systematical and untroubled. Although the Poles anticipated a German attack, they hoped that this would be limited in order to connect East Prussia with the *Reich*, thus eliminating the Polish Corridor and the status of the city of Danzig as a free state. This assessment proved to be wrong, and the attack caught the nation by surprise. The Western Allies did not intervene, although far reaching guarantees had been given. This was possibly due to grim memories of the disasterous mutual defense commitments, which inevitably led to the outbreak of World War I.

1 – 6 September 1939

Heeresgruppe Süd, with 14.Army, advanced through the Beskids Mountains and met with stiff resistance. This and the difficult terrain significantly slowed the initial rapid advance. The headwaters of the river Vistula near Krakow

Left:
The 7TP light tank was the mainstay of the Polish army and equipped the 1st and 2nd Light Tank Battalions. The vehicle was powered by a four-cylinder PZlnz.235 (Saurer VBLDd) diesel engine and was fabricated from riveted hardened steel. It mounted a 37mm Bofors wz.37 gun (which could defeat all German tanks including the PzKpfw IV) and a 7.92mm Ckm wz.30 machine gun. Although well-armed, armour protection was poor; a maximum of only 17mm on the front. (Getty)

were reached on 2 September, and on the same day, 20.Army managed to cross the river Warta. On 5 September, Kielce in central Poland was reached, and the Polish forces were driven back to the Warsaw region. On 6 September, Krakow was captured.

Heeresgruppe Nord advanced towards East Prussia, and at Tuchel and Graudenz a large Polish force was encircled and defeated after fierce battles. At Mlava, the Germans were temporarily halted. But after going around the right flank of the Polish positions, the Poles were forced to retreat and take new positions at the river Bug.

Facing the rapid advance of the Germans, the Polish forces were ordered to cross the rivers Bug, Vistula and Pillica and set up positions. However, the speed of the advancing *Panzerdivisionen* destroyed these plans.

7 – 18 September

Heeresgruppe Süd advanced via Tarnow and Przemysl to Lvov, and reached the river Bug on 9 September.

On 13 September, after heavy fighting, Radom in the central sector, 70km south of Warsaw, was captured after the Polish put up a stiff resistance. Five days later the outskirts of Warsaw were reached.

Above:
The PzKpfw II (left) has a white air-identification bar painted on the engine deck. Although the Luftwaffe held air superiority over the battlefield there was always the possibility of a sudden strike by Polish aircraft. (Prigent)

Heeresgruppe Nord

On 9 September, the forces *Heeresgruppe Nord* regrouped and encircled the cities of Warsaw and Modlin, and a large part of the Polish army was contained within this pocket. This caused the Polish government to flee to Romania on 18 September.

The German government declared victory, but the fighting continued. After *Heeresgruppe Nord* and *Süd* joined forces, the pocket around Warsaw and Modlin was divided. Subsequently, these were heavily attacked: Warsaw capitulated on 27 September, and Modlin on 28 September.

On 17 September, Stalin ordered to his forces to attack and to take his share of Poland. The invasion by Soviet forces in the east of the country was a further, final blow. The Poles finally realized that their country had been partitioned between two very hostile neighbours.

A German telex message, dated 17 September, describes the situation:

Russian Forces have crossed the border… and head towards Volhynia.

A further telex message, dated 29 September, reveals:

> In the course of planned moves over the line of demarcation, the German commander handed over the city of Przemysl to the Soviet troops.

The Republic of Poland had become history.

German tanks, an after action assessment

In general, the German tanks performed well. Many of the shortcomings known before outbreak of hostilities were finally verified in combat.

From the after action report, dated 1 October, 1939 from PzRgt 5:

Armament
The new machine gun has proven its worth and it is superior to the older type [MP 40 against MP 38, author]. The gun is most complicated and suffered repeatedly from jams. After special instructions from Insp.2 these shortcomings showed up only rarely. The 3.7cm gun had great accuracy and proved to be effective against enemy tanks. However, a high-explosive (HE) round which is effective against soft targets is desired. For reason of a stronger impact on the target we urge the introduction of a 5cm gun. The 7.5cm gun was extremely effective. In future this calibre will most certainly be the most important.

Below:
A PzKpfw I slowly moves forward to attack Polish troops positioned in houses and gardens. In the foreground an anti-tank team prepare their 3.7cm *Panzerabwehrkanone* (PaK) 35/36 for action; their towing vehicle, a Krupp 'Protze', is parked on the far side of the street. At that time the 3.7cm PaK 35/35 was powerful enough to destroy all enemy tanks of the day. (Anderson)

Above:
On 17 September 1939, Soviet troops crossed the border and advanced west. Here two T-26 tanks enter a Polish town; the leading tank is fitted with a machine gun mounted on the turret-top for air defence. The vehicle also has a a turret-mounted frame-type aerial, indicating that it is fitted with radio equipment. (Anderson)

Above:
The first encounters between German and Soviet troops were friendly. Here men of a German infantry unit gather around T-26 of the Red Army. (Münch)

Left:
Towards the end of the fighting in Poland a corridor was agreed for the safe movement of Soviet forces: a column of Red Army T-26 tanks passes a German *Schützenbattaillone* (motorcycle-mounted infantry). (Getty)

Above:
A PzKpfw II Ausf C being examined by German infantry, tanks were still something of a novelty on the battlefield in 1939. The tank still carries the very conspicuous white crosses, making it a clear target. (Anderson)

Right:
A column of PzKpfw II followed by a PzKpfw I *onhe Aufbau* (without bodywork); a type which was normally used as a driver-training vehicle. It is carrying a wooden section for temporary bridging, which suggests this particular tank is part of the *Panzer-Pionierkompanie* (PzPiKp – armoured engineers) in the division. (Münch)

A further report from the same source:

Armament
In general, our tank weapons are good. However, the magazine storage, especially in case of the *Kampfwagen* II is defective. The ammunition is prone to fouling. The 2cm magazines drop out of their racks in heavy terrain. On one occasion a full magazine ignited inside the tank…

It is interesting to note that by that time a standardization of guns was demanded, with the 7.5cm preferred as the main gun.

The current version of the PzKpfw III, the Ausf A to E, were only available in limited numbers at that time; but it was intended for it to become the most important type. Armed with a gun designed to defeat enemy tanks and having frontal-armour protection thick enough to withstand fire from anti-tank guns; it at last resembled a main combat tank.

A report, dated 13 December 1939, from PzRgt 1 reveals interesting information about their attitude towards the usability of the PzKpfw III:

On the orders of my regimental commander *Oberleutnant* Nedtwig, I report that the new PzKpfw III Ausf E is not ready for combat usage. Also that although the shortcomings reported on 22 November 1939 were remedied

Below:
The suspension on the PzKpfw II Ausf C, made up of five running wheels sprung by external leaf springs, work efficiently under normal conditions. The highly visible broad white cross marking has been neatly painted over by the crew of this tank. (Anderson)

Left:
A mixed column of German tanks parked on the market place of Lviv (Lemberg). The lead vehicle, a PzKpfw I Ausf B, carries a *Panzerwaffe*-style white skull painted on the front of the superstructure, below the white cross. Although the PzKpfw I was armed with a light machine gun and the PzKpfw II with a 2cm KwK 30/38 automatic cannon, both types performed better than expected against an inferior opponent. (Anderson)

by *Formänderungen* (product improvements), we still experience many breakdowns which confirm our above assessment.

The regiment has 28 PzKpfw III E and three gr PzBefWg available. These 31 vehicles have the same running gear, but we still have regular damage to the:

- Road wheels
- Steering unit
- Transmission
- Drive train

OKH has been repeatedly informed. An inspection by the responsible official, Heinrich Ernst Kniepkamp took place at the garrison. A number of *Formänderungen* were determined subsequently, and so far six improved PzKpfw III Ausf E have been returned to the regiment.

Two of these vehicles broke down during transit from the station to the garrison. Tank chassis No. 61108 had a damaged Variorex transmission; the complete vehicle had to be returned to Henschel again...

The problems listed above prove that the initial problems with the PzKpfw III Ausf E have still not been rectified. Furthermore, this version has difficult characteristics:

Below:
At the time, only PzAbt 67 was issued with the Czech-built PzKpfw 38(t) tanks. Both of these tanks have the aperture for the bow machine gun blanked-over, possibly they were being used as command tanks. (Anderson)

Exact positioning of the Panzer III Ausf E on a railway wagon is not possible, since the hydraulic clutch prevents such attempts.

A swift and smooth start is not possible by carefully releasing the clutch pedal, only by stepping on the accelerator. However, a definite jerk always occurs, which strains all components of the drive train and caused some breakages.

The tank cannot be tow-started, which is problematic in the winter season.

All discussions prove that the PzKpfw III Ausf E is still not as good as the PzKpfw III Ausf D…

The commander of the 1.PzDiv has added a comment under this report:

I agree to the comments of the commander of PzRgt 1. The new Panzer III Ausf E in their current state represents no advantage, but a danger to the troop.

Above:
A Czech-built PzKpfw 35(t) command tank, the large frame-type aerial was a typical fitting on all such modified vehicles. Due to the simple and rugged design of the suspension, the tank performed well in the early phase of the war. (Hoppe)

Tank tactics

In October 1939, the 3.PzDiv noted in an after action report to *Heeresgruppe Nord*:

1) Combat in a forest:
Facing a modern armed and well-trained enemy, the commitment of tanks in forested terrain can be possible only if it can be crossed on a broad front. The fragmented use of single tanks will inevitably lead to losses. Those battles which actually took place did not end up with losses only because the enemy was already beaten and on the run…

2) Combat in built-up areas:
In built-up areas the commitment of tanks must be avoided. In narrow streets, mobility is hindered. Furthermore, the crew´s observation means are insufficient. Dedicated enemy forces hiding in basements will be able to defeat our tanks. If at all, the tank must not drive in front of own infantry forces, but follow them after a good reconnaissance and then be used as a

support weapon. Fire from 7.5cm PzKpfw IV will be helpful; armoured vehicles can follow closely and eliminate resistance by the enemy in houses or on roofs.

Fighting in built-up areas in the west will be very different. While, due to their construction, houses in Polish villages quickly caught fire and burned down after direct hits from 7.5cm rounds, this will not happen in a western war with stronger-built houses…

3) Combat in darkness:
Combat with tanks during darkness has to be rejected. We noticed that at the despite their training, the accompanying infantry are nervous. Panic will lead to untargeted friendly fire…

Organizational changes

The concept of the *Panzerdivisionen* had been proven. However, it must be made clear that minor changes were incorporated on a more or less regular base: This of course depended heavily on the availability of equipment. As an example, during the invasion of Poland all *leichte Panzerkompanie* had a mixed establishment of tanks: PzKpfw I (two versions) and PzKpfw II (three

Below:
A *Panzerbefehlswagen* (PzBefWg) of 1.PzDiv, fitted with the conspicuous frame-type aerial. Based on the Ausf D, the vehicle has an eight-wheel running gear mounted on three bogies suspended on large leaf springs. (Hoppe)

Below:
The wreckage of a PzKpfw I after it was hit in the engine compartment by (most probably) an artillery shell, which destroyed the engine and ignited the fuel. (PeKo)

Left:
The main anti-tank
weapon used by Polish
forces was the 37mm
Bofors wz.37 cannon.
The performance of this
weapon was almost
comparable to that of
the German 3.7cm
Panzerabwehrkanone
(PaK), and was able to
fight any German tank
at ranges up to 500m.
(Getty)

Left:
The white cross painted
on the turrets of German
tanks for identification,
made an ideal aiming
point for Polish gunners.
The turret side of this
PzKpfw II, has received a
direct hit (Bofors 37mm)
which has penetrated
through the vision slot.
(Münch)

Above:
Suspension damage, caused by mines or enemy anti-tank guns, led to a tank being immobilized. Some could be quickly repaired in the field by the crew or a workshop team. Here the crew of a PzKpfw III Ausf E have replaced a damaged running wheel, and are attempting to refit the track. (Erdmann)

versions); the PzKpfw III was also available in four different *Ausführungen*. (Ausf) This caused severe problems with the supply of spare parts to over-stretched workshop units.

The end of the *leichte Divisionen*

The decision had been made to convert all *leichte Divisionen* (leDiv) to standard *Panzerdivisionen* before the invasion of Poland. The 1.leDiv merged with *PanzerAbteilung* (PzAbt) 65 which had already been reinforced with a complete *Panzerregiment* (PzRgt) 11. However, 2.leDiv, 3.leDiv, and 4.leDiv remained in their original organizational structure.

The 1.leDiv delivered an after action report, dated 4 October 1939, dealing with their experiences during the Polish campaign:

A. Technical state

The state of all motor vehicles require a longer stay in the home garrison, since only by using all our workshop and the manufacturer's capabilities will a quick and sufficient repair of all motor vehicles will be possible. The time

required for repairing the Panzers will take more than four weeks even if all spare parts are available. For all tanks and 50 percent of the *Zugmaschinen* (half-tracked tractors) new tracks will be needed. These ran without their rubber pads for a long time, ruining the mounts. Thus these tracks have to be completely replaced… When arriving at the loading stations, many tanks will have reached the 3,000km limit for the tracks: single links were already beginning to crack.

After reaching their garrison, *Panzerregiment* 11, including PzAbt 65, will be immobile. Apart from their tracks, the following numbers are still operational:

- 80 percent of the PzKpfw II
- 44 percent of the PzKpfw III
- 75 percent of the PzKpfw IV

B. Experiences

1) The fighting power of our troops does not meet that of 1914…
4) For the 1.leDiv the term *leichte Division* is misleading, since according its

Above:
A gantry has been erected at this temporary workshop site and has been used to remove the engine of this PzKpfw IV Ausf B. Note the engine cooling fans are visible on the opened engine hatch, also the magazines of machine-gun ammunition stacked on the roof of the turret. (PeKo)

Above:
A PzKpfw III Ausf E advances on a paved road, this version suffered from numerous teething problems, which forced the manufacturer (Daimler-Benz or MAN) to dispatch a task force of engineers to the front to repair the delicate Maybach Varioex transmission. As the war moved on the Panzer III becme a very reliable vehicle. (Hoppe)

1.leDiv losses	Armoured Cars	PzKpfw II	PzKpfw 35(t)	PzKpfw IV	PzBefWg
Complement	60	72	130	43	14
Total losses	9	8	69	9	8
Under repair	51	49	46	30	6
Available	–	15	15	4	–

These numbers seem to be surprising after the 'Feldzug der 18 Tage' (Campaign of 18 Days), as the German propaganda called the invasion of Poland. Despite having numerical superiority, the number of German vehicles lost seems to be high, especially for the PzKpfw 35(t): over 33 percent of the tanks were totally destroyed.

structure and equipment the unit is more or less equal to a normal *Panzerdivision*. This already led to misleading processing during the organization of the railway transport…

5) The *leichte Division* cannot cover the same sector an infantry division can … Usage of a *leichte Division* in wide areas with open flanks is possible only if the terrain will allow it or a weaked opponent is met.

6) Panzer:

The terrain did allow the commitment of the entire tank regiment only once (advance from Blonye to the river Vistula north of Warsaw). We could not gain any experience, since the enemy did not offer resistance… A close cooperation between own infantry and tanks did prove favourable. Especially the PzKpfw IV worked effectively, their fire was accurate and destructive against all targets.

The guns of the *Skodapanzer* [PzKpfw 35(t)] have to be provided with suitable fuses to enable them to engage infantry targets…

A great surprise during the first days was that an anti-tank hit does not necessarily result in the death of all crew members. Out of five hits only one will penetrate the armour. Such a penetration will in most cases lead to one casualty only; the driver and the wireless operator being most endangered.

Above:
A PzKpfw IV Ausf B parked alongside a *schwerer Achtradwagen* (heavy eight-wheeled armoured car – SdKfz 234) after a reconnaissance of the forward area. In 1940, the designation of this vehicle changed to SdKfz 232. (Anderson)

Above:
A column of PzKpfw IV of 1.PzDiv, some 50km south of Warsaw near the town of Tomaszów Mazowiecki. The leading four tanks are Ausf B, the last in the line, is an Ausf A. (Anderson)

This factor did improve morale among the crews.

When tanks were committed, singularly or in platoon strength, they will be susceptible to the flanks and will be rapidly knocked-out by hostile anti-tank defences…

The number of failed vehicles in need for repair was considerable (see the table on page 146). Some 131 from a total of 259 tanks broke down due to unspecified failures: the tracks began to fail when reaching 3,000km in service. This report by 1.leDiv provided the 'blueprint' for future improvements in the divisional workshop and supply services.

A further after action report of 2.leDiv unveils interesting details:

A. Organization:

1) The *leichte Division* has proved its value during the war in Poland. Its firepower was sufficient for the given tasks (during the advance to the Vistula). The main advantage lies in its far greater manoeuvrability,

when compared with the larger *Panzerdivision*, and for the possibility of quickly being transferred over longer distances (500km and more). For such a sudden move, the tanks must remain loaded on the trucks. The tank should be better protected with better armour. According to the limited tasks given to the unit, a complement of a smaller numbers of tanks has to be accepted… Attack power is lower when compared to a *Panzer* or *Infanteriedivision*, but nevertheless sufficient for the tasks stated above. *Leichte Divisionen* can also be used to assist attacking *Panzerdivisionen*…

2) *Panzerabteilung*: The Panzer I and II are not sufficiently armoured, and their firepower is too weak. The Polish anti-tank rifle was able to penetrate the frontal armour of the Panzer II at a range of 100m. We suggest re-equipping the *leichte Division* entirely with Panzer IV…

3) The signals battalion is not sufficient…

6) Each *leichte Division* must be provided with an anti-aircraft battalion equipped with self-propelled guns (two 3.7cm batteries, one 2cm battery)…

After the campaign, the *leichte Divisionen* were reorganized. The respective transport battalions were dispersed and their heavy trucks and trailers were sent to other units.

Below:
A battered PzKpfw II of PzRgt 7 shows approximately 20 clear penetrations. Examining their size, many could have been inflicted by fire from an anti-tank rifle or, more probably, a 20mm automatic cannon. (Münch)

- 1.*leichte Division* was re-designated as 6.*Panzerdivision*.
- 2.*leichte Division* was re-designated as 7.*Panzerdivision*. Additionally, PzRgt 25 was assigned to PzAbt 66.
- 3.*leichte Division* was re-designated as 8.*Panzerdivision*, and PzRgt 10 was assigned to PzAbt 67.
- 4.*leichte Division* was re-designated as 9.*Panzerdivision*. PzAbt 33 was re-organized as PzRgt 33.

On 9 October 1939, *Armeeoberkommando* (AOK) 8 (staff of the 8.Army) evaluated the course of the campaign.

I) Preliminary notice:

Noted below are experiences based on the special conditions of the Polish theatre of war: a war against an enemy, whose artillery was very inferior, and whose air force was barely seen in action. All experiences were influenced by eastern territorial conditions.

II) Experiences:

1) The German method, which attaches decisive importance on determined and courageous assault and combat utilizing combined

Above:
Tanks of 1.PzDiv advance on Polish forces positioned on the Bzura River. The lightly armoured PzKpfw I and IIs are led into the attack by a PzKpfw IV Ausf B, which had superior 30mm armour protection. (Anderson)

Left:
PzKpfw 35(t) tanks of 1.leDiv passes through a small stream. Shallow streams could be an advantage for a rapid advance, but had to be carefully reconnoitered as a bogged-down vehicle could halt an entire company. (Anderson)

Above:
The banner reads, 'We are Germans and commit ourselves to Adolf Hitler' as German PzKpfw II tanks pass through the gates of Danzig (Gdansk) and appear to be cheerfully welcomed by the people of the encircled city. (Anderson)

weapons, has proved to be effective. Wherever an assault failed, the reason was that many troops ignored these principles…

2) The impetus of the attack during the first days of combat, which intensified during the crossing of the river Warthe, slowed when the enemy's resistance grew stronger. This led to steady calls for support by other weapons (artillery, tanks). The expenditure of ammunition rose to an unhealthy proportion to the targets to be engaged…

3) The value of the troops is defined by the capability of its leaders. commanders and NCOs have to tough men…

4) Discipline is not perfect, as proved by several cases of looting…

10) Operating with the *Luftwaffe*

a) Cooperation with the reconnaissance squadrons ran smoothly…

b) The commitment of the operational *Luftwaffe* was of decisive importance for the army. The destruction of the railway and communications network paralyzed the Polish leadership. Attacks on supply columns limited the free movement of the Poles. A clear integration of the *Luftwaffe* combat squadrons under the army is regarded as being the best solution… The losses of own troops by friendly bombing at the river Bzura and at Warsaw did not improve the relationship between *Luftwaffe* and army…

III. Conclusion

The Polish campaign has been mounted under special conditions (a marginal
commitment of artillery, strong own air superiority, practically no Polish air attacks), which will not apply to the situation in a theatre of war in the west. Consequently the leadership and troops will have to switch to western conditions. It is desired that the time necessary for this change will be granted before a respective commitment is made, and avoid needless sacrifices…

However, time would show that Hitler was eager to progress with the planned attack on the Low Countries and then France, and ignored such reports and also his military commanders.

Below:
Following to the conclusion of the invasion of Poland, most German units were transferred back to the *Reich*. The people of Eisenach joyously welcome the tanks of PzRgt 2 back to their garrison in the town. In the background church of St George is visible. (Anderson)

CHAPTER 7

NORWAY: *UNTERNEHMEN WESERÜBUNG*

After the German victory over Poland, the political situation in Europe changed considerably. Britain and France had declared war on the German *Reich*, but to the surprise of the German leadership both nations renounced the use of military action.

However, Germany reviewed the many different scenarios which could affect the security and the economical situation of the *Reich*: Norway was at the forefront in these considerations.

For the *Kriegsmarine* (German Navy), the 'Great Belt' (Skagerrak) between Norway and Denmark, was essential as it was their gateway to the Atlantic. The establishment of strongholds along the Norwegian coast would allow submarines to be deployed directly into the North Atlantic, a matter of strategic importance (at that time nobody expected how quickly France would be beaten). Furthermore, German industry needed the iron ore from Norwegian mines and the *Reich* had serious doubts as to the true neutrality of Norway. In Britain plans were being made for closer involvement with the government in Oslo. The Russo-Finnish winter war provided the possibility; in order to deliver the weapons to support Finland it would be necessary to utilize the iron-ore railway.

The 'Altmark Incident' seemed to confirm this danger. The *Altmark* was a ship of the German merchant navy, which had onboard 300 rescued British sailors held as prisoners-of-war (POW). Returning from South America, the ship was spotted by HMS *Cossack* but escaped interception by entering Jossingfjord on the Norwegian coast. However, on 26 February 1940, HMS *Cossack* entered Norwegian 'neutral' waters and sent a boarding party to make a successful rescue. Germany now saw that it was necessary to

Above:
The PzAbtz (zbV) 40 (zbV – *zur besonderen Verwendung* – special duties) was reinforced by a heavy platoon, also known as *Panzerzug* Horstmann, issued with the three Krupp-built *Neubaufahrzeuge* (NbFz). The vehicle has a large elephant's head painted on the front slope of the superstructure. (Historyfacts)

plan a pre-emptive strike against Norway to avoid British forces occupying the country. It was called *Unternehmen Weserübung*.

Admiral Erich Raeder was to mastermind this operation, and his assessment is interesting as he described *Weserübung* as being contrary to all rules of warfare. Normally, for an undertaking of this scale full control of the seas around Norway was essential. However, the British fleet held absolute superiority in the Atlantic, assisted mainly by the severe lack of modern surface vessels in the *Kriegsmarine*; despite this, Raeder made the decision to order the operation. The exact timings for all parts of the operation were planned in total secrecy: Even Hermann Göring, as commander-in-chief of the *Luftwaffe*, was not included in the planning process.

The occupation was projected to be a peaceful operation allegedly to protect the neutrality of Denmark and Norway by some form of armed presence.

Strength of the *Panzerwaffe*, January 1940

PzKpfw I	838	PzKpfw II	1,010	PzKpfw III	150	PzKpfw IV	214
PzKpfw 35(t)	106	PzKpfw 38(t)	126	PzBefWg	203	**Total:**	**2,647**

Wesertag — the day of the attack

On 4 April 1940, Denmark was struck by a surprise attack, for which her forces were totally unprepared. After the general staff of the Danish Army was captured at their headquarters in Copenhagen, the government decided to accept German conditions for the surrender. The occupation was completed by 10 April.

On 7 April, several groups of *Kriegsmarine* warships left the German Bight and sailed north to attack the cities of Narvik, Trondheim, and Bergen. Oslo was an objective of both strategic and psychological importance. *Blücher*, the flagship of the *Kriegsmarine*, was sunk (*Lützow* was seriously damaged) off of Oslo by heavy fire from the 28cm guns (manufactured by Krupp) of Norwegian coastal batteries. On 10 April, Oslo was taken by German forces landed by transport aircraft at the city's airport. However, King Haakon and the Norwegian government had not been captured so the Norwegians, supported by French and British troops, decided to carry on fighting. Norway did not capitulate until 10 June 1940.

Although the *Kriegsmarine* had lost 33 per cent of its vessels, the Baltic Sea remained under German control and, of far greater importance, an unhindered access to supplies of iron ore.

Below:
One of the three NbFz in PzAbt (zbV) 40 being unloading from a freighter at Oslo docks on 19 April 1940. Due to their size, the vehicles attracted attention wherever they appeared. (Anderson)

Structure of a light Panzer Company (revised)

Gliederung der le PzKp
bei PzRgt 1,2,3,4,7,8 (1.,2. und 10. PzDiv)

Kp Trupp				
⊠	⊘	⊘	B	
1. Zug				
⊘	⊘	⊘	☐	☐
2. Zug				
⊘	⊘	⊘	☐	☐
3. Zug				
⊠	⊠	⊠		
4. Zug				
⊠	⊠	⊠		

☐	PzKpfw I
⊘	PzKpfw II
⊠	PzKpfw III
⊠ (t)	PzKpfw 38 (t)
⊠	PzKpfw IV
B	Kl PzBefw

Reallocation of the *Panzertruppe*

As noted earlier, the *leichte Divisionen* had been disbanded after the Polish campaign and reorganized as standard *Panzerdivisionen*. In late 1939, it was possible to equip a growing number of light companies with 3.7cm-armed tanks which were intended to fight against enemy armoured vehicles. This was possible partly due to an increase in production of the PzKpfw III, and that significant numbers of Czech-built PzKpfw 35(t) and 38(t) were available: a piece of good fortune for the *Panzerwaffe*.

The original *leichte Panzerkompanie* of 1937 was to have a complement of 17 PzKpfw III and five PzKpfw II. However, the number of 3.7cm armed tanks available was insufficient, so the average allocation per company was seven, and included eight PzKpfw II and four PzKpfw I. A large number of these vehicles were Czech-built tanks, so organizational structures were not always the same.

Panzers in Norway

An integral part of the German occupation of Norway was *Panzerzabteilung* (zbV) 40, (zbV – *zur besonderen Verwendung* – for special duties), a temporarily

Left:
Immediately after the unloading, the tanks of PzAbt (zbV) 40 were driven through the city of Oslo to their base.

Structure of a light Panzer Company (revised)

Gliederung der le PzKp
bei PzRgt 25 einschl. PzAbt 66 (7. PzDiv)

Kp Trupp

1. Zug

2. Zug

3. Zug

4. Zug

PzKpfw I
PzKpfw II
PzKpfw III
PzKpfw 38 (t)
PzKpfw IV
Kl PzBefw

Right:
Led by a kl PzBefWg and followed by a PzKpfw II, elements of PzAbt (zbV) 40 parades past their commanding officer in Oslo. (Anderson)

Structure of a light Panzer Company (revised)

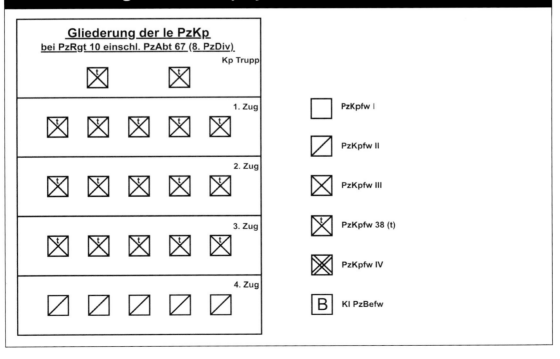

Gliederung der le PzKp
bei PzRgt 10 einschl. PzAbt 67 (8. PzDiv)

Kp Trupp

1. Zug

2. Zug

3. Zug

4. Zug

PzKpfw I

PzKpfw II

PzKpfw III

PzKpfw 38 (t)

PzKpfw IV

Kl PzBefw

Structure of a medium Panzer Company (revised)

Gliederung der m PzKp

bei PzRgt 1,2,3,4,7,8,10 (einschl. PzAbt 67)
und PzRgt 25 (einschl. PzAbt 66)

Kp Trupp

1. Zug

2. Zug xx)

3. Zug

PzKpfw I

PzKpfw II

PzKpfw III

PzKpfw 38 (t)

PzKpfw IV

Kl PzBefw

x) = bei PzRgt 10 und PzAbt 67 ohne kl PzBefWg
xx) = bei PzAbt 66 und 67 nur 3 PzKpfw IV

Above:
The Neubaufahrzeug (NbFz) mounted a 7.5cm and a 3.7cm in the main turret which allowed a wide variety of targets to be attacked. The machine guns mounted in the two auxiliary turrets were used against soft targets. (Historyfacts)

Right:
The armour on the NbFz was only 15 to 20mm thick. Here the crew has tried to improve protection for the machine-gun turret by using concrete blocks. However, enemy fire fractured the armour in front of the driver, and penetrated the mantlet. (Historyfacts)

established unit made up of three light companies equipped with PzKpfw I and II, taken from other *Panzerabteilungen*. In total, PzAbt (zbV) 40 was able to field 29 PzKpfw I, 18 PzKpfw II, four PzBefWg and three *Neubaufahrzeuge*.

This small detachment was split up to several smaller support units: apparently this was planned before the invasion, thus explaining the high number of command tanks. The *kleine Panzerbefehlswagen* (PzBefWg – command tanks) were used to ensure contact with the respective command staff. It is difficult to determine why German forces were not given light companies equipped with PzKpfw III and medium companies equipped with PzKfw IV: both types had been proven in Poland. Instead, the outdated *Neubaufahrzeuge* was chosen. One reason might be that supreme command did not want these more modern tanks to be seen in battle by French and British forces defending Norway. Furthermore, the original plan to attack Norway did not call for such sophisticated weaponry.

As the fighting proceeded the tanks of PzAbt (zbV) 40 proved to be of great value by providing valuable fire support for the ground troops.

Above:
A group of infantry seek cover behind a kl PzBefWg as it slowly advances. Although the tanks of PzAbt (zbV) 40 provided valuable fire support, the main burden of the fighting had to be carried out by the infantry. (bpk)

Above:
A kl PzBefwg at a local garage in the Norwegian mountains; long-range radio equipment was indispensable to German forces operating in the vast openness of the country. (Anderson)

After the Norwegian capitulation, the commander of unit wrote an after action report, excerpt:

> The enemy always had anti-tank guns at his disposal. In combat the British anti-tank gun [QF 2 pounder, author] and the French 25mm Hotchkiss were used. The armour on all tanks … was penetrated by both weapons…
>
> The deployment of tanks in mountain regions was limited by road and terrain conditions, also by the seasonal weather… Even during the summer a deployment away from beaten tracks was difficult… The experiences showed that groups of three tanks, headed by a PzKpfw II with the 2cm gun, were very effective. When fighting enemy units dug-in behind obstacles, the PzKpfw II proved to be very versatile. For combating defending artillery or anti-tank guns, the 2cm was an effective weapon… 2cm fire against rocks led to stone splinters, ending many missions… During deployments in cities, villages and even a single farmhouse, the enemy was quickly pushed back by 2cm

Above:
The PzKpfw II was a most precious weapon during the occupation of Norway. Due to the absence of a large enemy tank force, fire from the 2cm was sufficient to attack enemy positions. An anti-tank team, which has to haul their gun by hand, follows the slow-moving tank. (Prigent)

Above:
A PzKpfz II supports
German infantry patrolling
through the suburbs of
Oslo. (Getty)

fire. In most cases the buildings caught fire, which was unavoidable…
The *Neubaufahrzeuge* were deployed with great success even in the
mountains. Despite warnings in many official reports, all bridges, even
those with limitations of less than 5 tons, could be crossed without
problems. Also, the tanks could move through very narrow streets …
In most cases where *Neubaufahrzeuge* were sent forward, was where
our artillery could not be deployed. The tanks, however, were able to
fully compensate for the missing artillery… Effective fire was opened
with the 7.5cm gun, overpowering any enemy. While the 2cm gun was
effective, the 7.5cm high-explosive (HE) round had a truly destructive
impact… Firing of smoke shells, only possible by the 7.5cm gun of the
Neubaufahrzeug, was absolutely necessary to 'blind' the enemy and to
impede the use of his own weapons. For this reason the tank was

essential for combat in mountainous terrain. The fact that the tanks were widely spread out among varying combat groups, made supply with special ammunition (2cm, 7.5cm and tracer), and also with special rations [*Schokakola*, a chocolate/caffeine-based energy food] difficult…

These results are not surprising; indeed they were predictable (perhaps except the need for *Schokakola*). However, for the officials some important clues became obvious. The organizational structures, committing 7.5cm-armed tanks to the *mittlere Panzerkompanie* as integral part of any tank battalion, proved to be correct and far sighted. The 7.5cm gun, supplied with a selection of different ammunition (HE, AT, smoke) allowed a wide variety of targets to be successfully attacked.

It had also been observed that the armour on the German tanks was easily penetrated by any light anti-tank gun (even a portable anti-tank rifle). In 1930, most infantry forces were equipped with 7.92mm weapons firing armour-piercing (AP) rounds capable of penetrating 10mm steel, and it became obvious that tanks would have to be fitted with armour strong enough to withstand this fire. German tanks, including the PzKpfw IV Ausf A (the first production batch), had armour 14.5mm (maximum) thick. Even if more powerful anti-tank weapons became available, a

Below:
One *Neubaufahrzeug* (NbFz) was lost during the invasion of in Norway, after becoming bogged-down and was then blown up. The crew of this surviving NbFz has written their names on the side of the turret. (Hoppe)

Below:
The *Neubaufahrzeug* (NbFz) was only ever used for combat in the invasion of Norway. The combination of a 3.7cm gun against armoured targets and a 7.5cm gun for direct-fire support proved to work surprisingly well. (Anderson)

breakthrough by a tank battalion through positions held by an infantry division would be possible.

However, in the late 1930s this thinking had begun to change, and a new way of thinking developed. This especially applied to the PzKpfw III, when it was decided that it should be built with armour strong enough to withstand fire from any weapon with a calibre of 3.7cm. Therefore, the proposed increase in frontal armour on most German tanks had begun before the Polish campaign. The more recent PzKpfw IV versions (Ausf B and C), also PzKpfw III Ausf E, were fitted with frontal armour increased to 30mm thick which gave adequate protection against 2cm automatic guns. This decision seemed to have been expedient, although the enemy anti-tank guns noted above were still able to penetrate this armour at close range. Interestingly, the first *Sturmgeschütz* assault guns were issued to the troop at that time. These vehicles, with 50mm frontal armour, proved to be immune to fire from 2.5cm weapons.

By 1940, it was impossible to absolutely protect an armoured vehicle and still maintain its mobility on the battlefield: any increase to the armour will result in an increase in weight.

Since German military planners put great emphasis on mobile warfare, an ideal had to be sought. The notion of a slow moving, heavily-armoured infantry tank was no longer valid, speed was the decisive factor – not only the speed of the tanks, but the speed of decision making by German military and political their leaders.

However, front-line experiences led to a large-scale *Panzerverstärkungs-Programm*. Thicker armour was retro-fitted to German tanks already in service, and the same improvements were made to all tanks on the production line. Originally, the ZW was designed as a 12-ton class tank, and fitted with a drive train suitable for this weight. The first production vehicles (Ausf A) weighed 15t: in 1940, the weight of a PzKpfw III Ausf E had increased to 19.5t.

Above:
Although the PzKpfw I was outclassed by 1940 standards, it was employed with some success in Norway. However, if fired on by a British Ordnance QF 2-pounder or French 25mm anti-tank gun the PzKpfw I, and all other German tanks of the time, would be in severe danger. (Getty)

CHAPTER 8

THE WESTERN CAMPAIGN

The cynical German principle of creating *Lebensraum im Osten* (living space in the east) for the German people was the basis of the national socialist ideology, which dated back to the 1920s. To achieve this it would be necessary to invade and occupy large areas of the Soviet Union. However, Adolf Hitler and his cohorts considered the Western democracies (in particular France) as a hindrance which would have to be eliminated before any attack to the east.

In late 1938, the policy of appeasement, promoted by Britain and France, had totally failed: their passive toleration had allowed Hitler to build up his armed forces and to prepare his plans for more territorial conquests. With the German 'seizure of Prague' and their occupation of Czechoslovakia, the Western allies finally awoke to the reality of a war in Europe.

After the successful invasion of Poland, the *Westfeldzug* (Western Campaign) was being planned. Principally, this was almost identical to the Schlieffen plan from World War I: a pincer movement in which German troops were to advance down through Belgium to cross the French border, while the right flank of their forces would advance to Paris and encircle the city.

This uninspired plan ignored recent experience in other battles. The civil war in Spain was decided, despite Franco's superiority in arms and troops, after three long years of bitter fighting. Even the mighty Soviet army was unable to quickly overcome Finnish resistance in the winter war of 1939/40. Was the German idea of overwhelming an opponent by combined ground and air operations, spearheaded by dedicated tank units, practical?

Left:
A PzKpfw IV Ausf B from the 6.PzDiv passes through an occupied French town. The Ausf B and C were the only versions not fitted a hull machine gun. The crew has fitted track links to the front of the vehicle, in an attempt to reinforce the frontal armour. (Historyfacts)

Above:
France relied on the
Maginot Line, a system of
bunkers and fortifications
that ran the length of the
Franco-German border.
French military planners
were confident that it
would be impossible for
enemy formations to break
through and advance
into the heart of France.
(Anderson)

Right:
The line was built with
hundreds of bunkers
and gun emplacements,
for machine guns and
artillery, to repel any
'standard pattern'
of attack by infantry
supported by armour and
artillery. (Anderson)

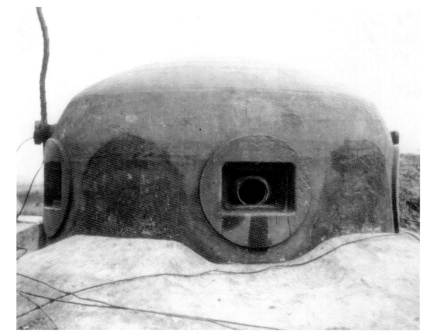

The 'impenetrable' Maginot Line

After the catastrophe of World War I, the French government decided to adopt a more or less passive stance to assure '*la Defence de la Nation*'. Inspired, or better soothed by the myth of Verdun – this very fortress on the river Maas which in 1916 withstood attacks by superior German forces – a line of massive defences was planned. The Maginot Line, named after André Maginot the French Minister of War, was made up of more than 100 artillery fortresses supplemented with hundreds of smaller bunkers and gun positions. This impressive defensive line on the eastern borders France stretched from the Mediterranean Sea to the Ardennes forest.

The system had weaknesses: More than 30 divisions of troops would be required to man the emplacements ready for battle (these forces could not be used for conventional infantry combat), including mobile defence. Due to the extraordinary cost of construction, not all components of the line were completed; there were many undefended gaps when the Germans attacked.

Even after the German invasion of Poland, the French felt safe behind their fortified borders. If the Germans were unable to overcome the Maginot Line and the Ardennes region, they would be forced to attack

Above:
In May 1940, the basically identical PzKpfw III Ausf E and F became available in larger numbers (349). Most of the basic mechanical problems had been solved, but the delicate Maybach Varioex transmission continued to be unreliable. The grinning devil's head, visible on the turret side, is the emblem of PzRgt 31. (Anderson)

Above:
Tanks of 4.PzDiv – two PzKpfw II and a PzKpfw III Ausf E – move through a village. From experience gained after combat in Poland, the distinctive white cross was replaced by a simple white-outlined cross. The vehicle number was painted on a small rhomboid-shaped plate (according to the regulations) and repeated in larger numerals on the turret for easier identification. (Zimmermann)

through the Netherlands and Belgium. However, the French army was confident that it could repeat the action of World War I and halt and defeat the aggressor.

'Sitzkrieg' — the phoney war

The 'Sitzkrieg', was the period of deceptive calm in the months following the British and French declaration of war against the German *Reich* on 3 September 1939. While Germany had already finalized plans to attack; France, the Netherlands, and Belgium had not prepared a mutual defensive strategy. During this period, there were several limited skirmishes on the border between France and German. The most significant was the Saar offensive. On 7 September, in an attempt to test the state of the German defences, French troops occupied parts of the Saarland. This half-hearted advance ended on 16 September, when the French government decided to switch to purely defensive tactics, but the tense situation continued through the winter of 1939/40.

In March 1940, disaster struck when a German military transport aircraft drifted off course and was forced to land in Belgium. Known as the 'Mechelen Incident', a German officer on the aircraft carried a full set of unencrypted documents, detailing the offensive operations, which were confiscated by the Belgians. But, despite the importance of the contents, neither France nor Britain took the matter seriously.

The 'sickle'

After the 'Mechelen Incident', German military planners were forced to prepare new plans for the attack on France. This was the tasked to General Erich von Manstein who, supported by Guderian, favoured a different solution. Both officers realized that only a quick and deliberate attack could bring a decision. There was a great danger that if German forces could not receive reserves and supplies they would become depleted and the impetus of the invasion would be halted resulting in a static battlefront.

General von Manstein was aware of where the Western armies were deployed; most of their best forces were concentrated on the French–Belgian border, but many units were needlessly positioned along the Maginot Line. The General decided not attack them front on from the north with all of his forces, but instead use only five of his ten available *Panzerdivisionen* to cross through the Netherlands and Belgium. The remaining five *Panzerdivisionen* were to be deployed for the advance through Luxemburg and into the Ardennes. However, this last part of his plan was indeed unrealistic as it was thought that it would be virtually impossible to move large tank formations along the narrow tracks through mountain forests.

General von Manstein's 'sickle' was to then advance west in order to reach the channel coast at Calais, thus cutting off Allied forces. Wherever possible during the assault, Panzer units would attack any enemy forces encountered to the sides of the advance. The *Panzerdivisionen* attacking the Netherlands and Belgium had to fight against French army and troops of the British Expeditionary Forces (BEF). It would be only a matter of time before these troops were cut-off and annihilated.

Preparing for action:

In March 1940, the AOK 6 determined:

To Heeresgruppe B

The fighting power and state of training in the 3.PzDiv and 4.PzDiv subordinated under 6.Army give rise to particular concern, as to whether the divisions can still fulfill their assigned tasks.

Above:
A PzKpfw IV of PzRgt 31, (5.PzDiv): The devil's head emblem is clearly visible on the side of the turret. The official divisional emblem is stencilled on the superstructure to the right of the cross. (Anderson)

Above:
French children take the opportunity to examine PzKpfw III Ausf F tanks of PzRgt 5 (3.PzDiv) during a halt on a village road. The vehicles are partially camouflaged with foliage and recovery cables shackled to the towing eyes. (Hoppe)

Left:
A PzKpfw I, *Filmpanzer* (camera tank) from a propaganda unit, attached to the light platoon of battalion, which was used to film combat action. The tank carries a fascine (a bundle of wooden poles) on the engine deck for filling shallow obstacles. (NARA)

1) The deficiencies of fighting power are due for the following reasons:

a) The PzKpfw III (3.7cm) is inferior to the tanks of the Western opponents (4.7cm) in terms of quantity of weapons.
b) By order of OKH... dated 21 February 1940, for the 3. and the 4.PzDiv a considerably unfavourable equipping with tanks was decreed.
c) 3. and 4.PzDiv were ordered to submit one lePzKp each without holding out the prospect of replacements...
d) Insufficient equipment with anti-tank weapons: 3. and 4.PzDiv have only one anti-tank battalion with two companies each.

The state of the training has worsened due to the following reasons:
a) Since their relocation to the western border, the divisions were not able to hold combat exercises or firing practice.
b) Since end of the Polish campaign numerous company and platoon leaders were exchanged. Up to 25 percent of the NCOs and enlisted men have no combat experience...
c) The strong limitation on fuel consumption complicates training significantly... Only half of the allotted fuel supply was available...

Below:
The 4.PzDiv had only 40 PzKPfw III in its four *Abteilungen*, five per light company, although the vast majority were PzKpfw I and II. The divisional marking is painted on the front of the superstructure. (Erdmann)

Above:
A company of PzKpfw
III Ausf F tanks of PzRgt
5 (3.PzDiv) during halt
on a paved road. Two
ventilation vents, a
distinctive feature in of
the Ausf E, were fitted to
improve cooling to the
Varioex transmission.
(Hoppe)

This call for help describes the parlous state, at least for several units, of the *Panzerwaffe*. Was the German war machine ready for the great challenge required in the war plans of Adolf Hitler?

The situation regarding the quality of the war material was not without problems. The German authorities had known for a long time that the ballistic performance of the 3.7cm armament for the proposed PzKpfw III was insufficient to fight against French armour. The installation of a 5cm gun (as discussed earlier), would possibly have given the Germans a certain advantage. However, due to the slow rate at which the PzKpfw III was being introduced into service, a change to this more potent weapon would certainly have resulted in further delays.

The *Panzerkampfwagen* (PzKpfw) IV, *Begleitwagen* (escort tank), was originally designed as direct-fire support. When development of the *Begleitwagen* began it was thought that strong frontal armour protection was of secondary importance. However before 1939, it was decided to increase frontal armour from 14.5mm (Ausf A, only 35 built) to 30mm. This decision possibly originated from intelligence reports written after action against French armoured forces.

Left:
Tanks of 4.PzDiv prepare
for the attack in a field
of new corn. Of the 16
tanks visible, only three
are medium tanks suitably
armed for combat against
French or British tanks.
(Zimmermann)

Strength of the *Panzerwaffe*, May 1940							
PzKpfw I	1,077	PzKpfw II	1,042	PzKpfw III	381	PzKpfw IV	290
PzKpfw 35(t)	143	PzKpfw 38(t)	238	PzBefWg	244	**Total:**	**3,465**

Below:
A PzKpfw III from 1.PzDiv being refuelled by its crew, the filler pipe for the fuel tank was positioned in the engine compartment. The *Panzerwaffe* relied on simple ('Jerry') cans for the transportation of fuel. Very easy to transport, the method was far superior to the use of the vulnerable fuel-tanker trucks used by the British and French. (NARA)

The shortage of basic supplies such as fuel seems to be more fatal. Although there is little known regarding problems with the fuel supply during the western campaign, the incidents mentioned above were certainly a cause for concern. Germany was a country with very limited supplies of raw materials which, by 1940, were certainly insufficient to support a longer conflict.

In January 1940, the slow production of more powerful tanks made the planned (dated 1937) equipping of each *Panzerdivision* with 128 PzKpfw III and 56 PzKpfw IV impossible. For instance, 1.PzDiv had 58 PzKpfw III and 40 PzKpfw IV. The 4.PzDiv (see above), had 40 PzKpfw III and 24 PzKpfw IV (these are approximate figures, depending on actual equipment, technical failures, etc. and excluding command tanks). The missing vehicles were substituted by light tanks.

Fall Gelb (Plan Yellow) — breakthrough to the Channel

On 10 May 1940, troops of 3.PzDiv and 4.PzDiv crossed the German border at Aachen and into Belgium, their objective Charleroi. Further to the south, 5.PzDiv and 7.PzDiv began to advance through Belgium. These four divisions had led the attack against the main part of the BEF and French forces. In the north, 9.PzDiv advanced through the Netherlands. Now all Allied units in the Low Countries were involved in attempting to halt the German attack.

From the recollections of *Hauptmann* Schneider-Kolstalski, 2./PzRgt 6, 3.PzDiv:

So, today is the great day, we have to prove ourselves in the west… Returning to the company, I notice that a French tank was brought in, a R35… It is the first time I have seen a modern French tank. We are stunned by the thick armour, I am getting thoughtful. After the only 3.7cm armed tank in the company had dropped out due to a mechanical failure, my company has only 2cm guns to defeat enemy tanks… The enemy has at least 3.7cm guns… The only opportunity for us is to get near the enemy tank to open fire at the vertical plates or hatches…

Below:
Men of the famous 7.PzDiv mount their PzKpfw 38(t) tanks. These light and manoeuvrable fast tanks allowed Rommel to advance his forces several hundred kilometres each day. (NARA)

… My driver tries to smash down an iron-barred gate. Sadly, the 2cm gun gets stuck while trying, and now we have to use the sledgehammer to remove the gate, while the bullets fly around our ears…

… Driving around a corner, I spot the barrel of an anti-tank gun at 70m range. Two Frenchman jump behind their armour shield and aim at us; I am faster and open fire. The anti-tank gun's shield shows four round holes, after a short burst of fire from our machine gun the crew surrenders. Now French soldiers come from all direction, raising their hands…

… Suddenly the men shout: 'Tanks' At a distance of 600m two PzKpfw III of the 4.Kp open fire. Although we observe many clear hits, their rounds fail to penetrate… Suddenly an R35 appears from the right at 80m. The muzzle of its 3.7cm gun slowly moves on to my tank. I fire a complete magazine 2cm shells. The tank stops, giving off smoke. I cannot see any penetration…

… After driving around a bend, another R35 heads directly towards me… I fire half a magazine with remarkable success. The impact of my fire is so high that the driver's hatch shears off. I send a burst of machine-gun fire at the opening… After passing the tank, the same fight takes place with another tank. A third R35 however, cannot be stopped this way. All my rounds bounce off; I do not know what to do. If he opens fire with his 3.7cm gun, he will finish us off. Fortunately the rear hatch opens, and two arms waving a white flag appear. Two well-fed Paris citizens, at least 35 years-old, leave the tank …

Suddenly the ravine opens on to a wide field, I hear heavy machine-gun fire. My transmitter fails, and I can lead the company only by signals and example. We cannot stop here, so we move on in the line of attack. To the left a heavy French tank appears, type Somua… Since I am faster, I drive around a hump to bypass him, and get to his rear. I follow him at 20m, but he does not notice us…. I fire ten grenades at his rear, but despite a strong eruption of smoke he moves on. Before the tank can turn his turret towards us, my driver quickly reacts and our tank disappears behind another hump. At this moment I notice a hard strike and hear my driver shouting: 'Engine stalled, anti-tank gun hit'. We bail out of our trusted tank…

In this report Schneider-Kostalski describes the problems both sides had in combat during the first assault. Beside the fact that the 6.PzDiv had only 42 PzKpfw III and 26 PzKpfw IV, the German tanks proved to be under-gunned. Firing the standard 3.7cm *Panzergrenate* (PzGr – armour-piercing [AP] round), the PzKpfw could not penetrate the 35 to 40mm thick armour on the Renault R35 or Somua S35. Schneider-Kostalski details his engagements with the heavily-armoured French infantry tanks which were destroyed or neutralized by lucky shots at close range by automatic fire from his 2cm gun. The S35, however, having fewer weak points (access hatch), proved to be immune to 2cm and 3.7cm fire.

Above:
A PzKpfw I passes through a captured French Army control point near the town of Avenes-sur-Helpe some 14km from the border of Belgium on 4 June 1940. (bpk)

Rommel – full steam

The famous 7.*Panzerdivision* (34 PzKpfw I, 68 PzKpfw II, 91 PzKpfw 38(t), and 24 PzKPfw IV) crossed the border south of Köln (Cologne) on 10 May 1940, and two days later they reached the river Maas (Meuse) at Dinant. After heavy fighting the river was crossed, and several counterattacks were repulsed over the next two days. On 17 May, the French border fortifications were breached. On 19 May, Arras was reached and Cambrai taken. On 21 May, a massive counterattack by the BEF was successfully repulsed, but 7.PzDiv recorded heavy losses. The La Bassée–Bethune canal near Lille was a serious obstacle; on 27 May two portable bridges were erected. After some days at rest, the divisions headed towards the river Somme, which was crossed on 5 June. Rouen was taken four days later, and the Atlantic coast was reached in July 1940.

After the campaign the unit delivered answers to a questionnaire, excerpt:

The French anti-tank units and the crews of the French tanks performed well, they inflicted severe losses on our troop. The British soldier fought tougher and more doggedly than the French… Our troop was at no time surprised by any new fighting method…

The division was very successful, reaching the daily objectives as rapidly as possible; the tank regiment was always in the first line. At nearly every opportunity the tank assault was closely followed by reconnaissance sections, motor-cycle units, motorized infantry, the artillery, the tank destroyers and light and heavy Flak guns…

… Much experience was gained during combat against enemy tanks. Regarding their armour protection, the enemy tanks proved to be far superior in most cases. By opening of fire early and rapid advance to suited positions, even stronger tanks were overpowered…

…Wherever enemy tank assaults were successful against own rifle units (Arras, St Eloy and at the La Basée canal), this was possible only due to the fact that the 3.7cm PaK had proven absolutely inadequate against the strong French and British tanks. Occasionally light and heavy Flak batteries and a field howitzer battery were subordinated under the rifle unit… The allotment of artillery to the rifle units has proved its worth, but weakened the divisional artillery…

Below:
PzKpfw III of an unidentified unit cross a pontoon bridge over a canal somewhere on the western front in 1940. The rapid assembly of portable pontoon bridges was a decisive for the speed of the continued advance. (Anderson)

Left:
A PzKpfw 35(t) and PzKpfw II of 6.PzDiv use a pontoon ferry to cross the river Meuse (Maas) at Montherné in the Ardennes on 14 May 1940. (bpk)

Below:
Erwin Rommel, the commander of 7.PzDiv, discusses the situation on the battlefront with his senior officers. Their 'desk' is the bonnet (hood) of an SdKfz 247 Ausf A (the armoured version of the Krupp 'Protze') staff vehicle which carried long-range radio equipment. (Anderson)

… As a lead division, the 7.PzDiv was far ahead of the front during a longer period. As anticipated, the unit became an easy victim of enemy bombers and strafing aircraft. Since the division's anti-aircraft elements were necessarily assigned for defence against enemy tanks, their own anti-aircraft weapons were insufficient… The division had days when it was the target for enemy air raids from early morning until late afternoon, without seeing a *Luftwaffe* aircraft in the air…

… Our principles regarding leadership and combat with armoured units was generally proven. The daily capacity given for a tank division was on some days exceeded by far. Furthermore, during the fighting very high average speeds were achieved. The peak performance was 340km in one day…

… Night attacks proved especially successful during the breakthrough of the Maginot Line, whenever the unit met resistance during these raids, the enemy was overrun by firing from all guns…

.. It was of utmost importance that the divisional commander was far at the front with his staff… it is necessary to assign armoured vehicle to the staff platoon including the signals section…

… The fighting power of a *Panzerdivison* according previous structures is sufficient… The division, however, prefers structuring of the *Panzerregiment* with two *Abteilungen* at four companies instead of three *Abteilungen* at three companies each. Thus it is easier to submit a support company for the rifle regiment without depleting the *Abteilung*'s fire power…

… The German *Panzerkampfwagen* has good weapons and very good observation means. In these aspects they are superior to the French and the British tanks. The division is sure that the German tank is faster than the French or British. It is possible that this conclusion was drawn because the divisions´ tank assaults were always driven at utmost speed. The chassis of the PzKpfw 38(t) has proven to be reliable and durable, and is, in this regard, superior to all German types. At three consecutive days of marches up to 280km each, the number of PzKpfw 38(t) having failed to technical problems was marginal. However, all tanks of the division offer protection against infantry armour-piercing bullets only; they are not safe against fire from anti-tank rifles and the 25mm anti-tank gun.

Evaluation

On 27 May, a large-scale tank attack was prepared. The 7.PzDiv, reinforced by 8.PzBrig (PzRgt 15 and PzRgt 31 of 5.PzDiv) was ordered to advance to La Bassée. By early afternoon, parts of 7.PzDiv had already crossed the canal and by 16.30hrs, the last elements of PzRgt 25 had reached the La Bassée to Estaires road. Single British tanks were destroyed by German heavy tanks (PzKpfw IV) to safeguard the assembly area. At 17.45hrs, PzRgt 31 managed to cross the canal and the attack was subsequently ordered; 15 minutes later 400 tanks launch the attack:

Own artillery covers the right flank against La Bassée and lays a smoke screen. What an impressive experience to move forward in this iron box: the commanders peep out of their cupolas and observe. The gunners aim at the assigned targets… First radio messages report the destruction of enemy tanks… We reach the first objective, the heights at Fournes…. In Fournes we meet retreating enemy columns. Ammunition vehicles and fuel tankers explode; brightly-coloured flames illuminate targets for our tanks. At 24.00hrs, the tanks coming from rest points arrive. It is a view of strange

Above:
Other than the British A12 Infantry Tank Mk II (Matilda II), the French B1 was the heaviest-armoured tank the German forces had to face. The type had 60mm frontal amour which proved to be impervious to fire from any German tank. (Anderson)

Right:
The French medium tank Somua S35 was a cavalry tank with excellent performance. Armed with the same 47mm gun as the B1 (the turrets were identical), it had 50mm-thick armour (Anderson)

Above:
In 1940, France had a large number of Renault R35 and the Hotchkiss H35 infantry tanks, both armed with the 37mm gun. Although having better armour than German tanks, their combat value was very limited due to both types having a two-man crew, inadequate vision and a low road speed. (Anderson)

Left:
A captured British A12 Infantry Tank Mk II (Matilda II) 'Gorgonzola' being inspected by men from a *Schützebataillone* (motorcycle infantry battalion). (Anderson)

Above:
The *Panzerpionier-Kompanie* (PzPiKp – armoured engineer company) of 7.PzDiv was issued with specialized vehicles often built on the chassis of obsolete tanks. The first and the third tank are *Brückenleger* II, simple bridge-laying vehicles based on the hull of the PzKpfw II. The vehicle in the centre is a PzKpfw I *Ladungsleger* (explosive-charge carrier). (Anderson)

beauty to observe the tracers in the darkness of night. Burning columns of vehicles, houses and haystacks lead the advance. Enemy anti-tank fire, aimlessly fired from great distances, has no effect...

During the same night a *Panzerabteilung* advances to reach the main retreat road of the opponent...

PzRgt 3 of 2.PzDiv was among the units chosen to cross into the Ardennes from Luxemburg. After the regiment had crossed the river Maas (Meuse) it continued to advance to the west reaching St.Quentin from where these reports were sent:

18 May 1940.
Between Bellenglise and Pontru, *Kradschützen* (motor-cycle troops) suffered heavy casualties from fire by a single B1. The tank retreated northwest. The fifth company was ordered to search and find the tank. It was found in Jeancourt, abandoned by its crew. The tank was set on fire by an 8.8cm FlaK. Firing tests revealed that the 3.7cm PaK cannot penetrate the armour of this tank at ranges of 100m...

A report by *Oberleutnant* Hingst, of 8./PzRgt 3, dated 19 May 1940:

I fired at a French Hotchkiss 3.7cm tank from my PzKpfw IV, using a 7.5cm PzGr at 450m. The second round hit the tank between and turret

and hull superstructure. The turret was totally ripped off of its mounting, and a small hole emerged in the roof plate… Another round hit the hull (cast steel, rounded) at an angle of 50°, the only damage was a 2mm deep and 10cm long scrape…

The 1.PzDiv advanced alongside the 2.PzDiv. From an 8./PzRgt 1 after-action report dated 24 May 1940 at St Folquin:

The 2.Platoon of 4.Kp, subordinated to 8.Kp, is ordered to support the riflemen expanding the bridgehead. The reconnaissance for this operation will be enforced in the forenoon by *Leutnant* von Villebois and *Leutnant* Lucas.
Execution: The first canal, which was already taken the day before, is being crossed without problems. The tanks give covering fire for the

Above:
Two tanks of 7.PzDiv move into jump off positions. The first three platoons of the light company were equipped with PzKPfw 38(t). Those in 4.PzDiv were equipped with PzKpfw II. (NARA)

Right:
General Heinz Guderian, commanded the XIX *Armeekorps* during the French campaign, and proved his concept of using the combined commitment of tank forces and infantry was possible. Like Rommel, he was highly popular among his men who he led the front. (Anderson)

Above:
The bison emblem painted on the turret side identifies this tank as a PzKpfw III Ausf E of PzRgt 7, 10.PzDiv. The single-digit number is unusual, possibly the tank is from the staff section of the *Abteilung*. The rods protruding out of the ventilation slots on the engine bay cover are replacement track pins. (Anderson)

Left:
A PzKpfw IV from 1.PzDiv one of the three tank divisions commanded by General Guderian. The PzKpfw IV (along with the PzKpfw III) was the mainstay of the *Panzerwaffe*. The type mounted a very effective 7.5cm short-barreled gun. (Anderson)

Above:
Three PzKpfw II of 6.PzDiv followed by a PzKpfw 35(t) are carrying swastika flags as an air-recognition aid for pilots of the *Luftwaffe*. (Anderson)

riflemen to advance to the second canal. Then the tanks drive to the canal giving further support during the crossing and the expansion of the landing area. Initially the advance happens swiftly, but stagnates because the riflemen have to use rubber dinghies. The PzKpfw IV shoot down one house after another occupied by French machine-gun teams firing high-explosive rounds fitted with time delay. During this operation the crews of the PzKpfw IV mastered a true artillery mission with bravery and skill; the riflemen could then expand their bridgehead without further losses.

An after-action report from PzRgt 33 of 9.PzDiv, gives an interesting account of a tank-versus-tank battle between a PzKpfw IV and a French B1 heavy tank:

On 16 June 1940, the regiment was halted on the highway for a short rest. Suddenly, we were called up by the order 'prepare for action, there is a heavy tank just ahead of us – fire at once.' Due to the dust, I was unable to recognize anything through the aiming devices, but I fired as best I could in the indicated direction. This round burst 150m ahead of us and I learned later that it had demolished a wine shop adjacent to the

Above:
Captured equipment in Belgium: a 47mm T-13 light tank destroyer based on the chassis of a Vickers Carden Loyd light tank alongside a Vickers utility tractor. (Anderson)

French tank. After the dust had cleared a little, the outline of the heavy tank loomed up, and the situation came to a showdown. My loader worked without interruption. Three PzGr were fired in succession into the front of the enemy tank, causing it to cease fighting and turn back... As we advanced we saw another B1 tank just ahead of us. I estimated the range to be 600m and opened fire. The first round fell short, but the next six rounds hit the side of the French tank. I ceased fire when we reached the depression at the foot of the hill...

... Suddenly, the battalion commander gave the following order: 'Halt. Heavy tank at eleven o'clock'... I estimated the range quickly, but carefully, and made adjustments. Finally, I fired and the projectiles flew like a ball of fire against the French tank, hurling a piece of its track high into the air. The loader shouted. ("No more ammunition") The driver immediately sensed the dangerous situation we were in and let the tank roll back a few metres into cover. Luckily, the driver found three more rounds of PzGr, which were passed quickly to the loader and fired at the enemy. These three rounds silenced the French tank, so we drove forward and examined our victim. Its crew, including a lieutenant colonel, dismounted and surrendered.

Above:
The crew of this PzKpfw IV Ausf A of 1.PzDiv has added spare tracks to the front of their tank in order to reinforce the thin 14.5mm armour. Large swastika flags, for air-recognition, are spread over the engine cover of the tank and also laid out over the field. (NARA)

For the *Panzerwaffe*, the PzKpfw IV was of great importance. Unlike most other guns installed in tanks of that period, the 7.5cm KwK fired a great variety of ammunition, including smoke and effective HE rounds which allowed a wide range of objectives to be engaged. Although the 7.5cm KwK was the only tank gun able to deal with French heavy armour, the penetration of armour plates was not superior due to a low muzzle velocity (385mps). However, the pure impact of a direct hit could blow off or cause a turret to seize.

The Western Campaign – assessing the Panzer

As stated above, the German *Panzerwaffe* was to be issued with the PzKpfw III as the main tank for the *Panzerdivisionen*, and by 1940 some 380 were available. The PzKpfw IV was designed as an escort tank. However, the type was more capable and from 1942 it became the prime battle tank; the true backbone of the *Panzerwaffe*. Luckily for the Germans, large numbers of Czech-built PzKpfw 35(t) and 38(t) were available to replace the PzKpfw III, allowing the establishment of three additional *Panzerdivisionen* equipped with these types.

The requirements for a tank suitable for operational missions comprised firepower, mobility and armour protection. The firepower is influenced by the sheer effect of the weapon defined by its muzzle velocity, types of ammunition and the rate of fire. The latter variable is heavily influenced by the type and quality of the crew's sighting and observation equipment; the ammunition (one- or two-piece, weight and dimensions), the construction of the gun (fully or semi-automatic, or manual operation), the space inside the tank and finally the division of tasks in the crew.

Mobility depends on a high average speed combined with good acceleration. Of great importance is the design of the transmission and engine performance. High manoeuvrability requires a well-designed steering system to enable tight turns in a small place. The range of the vehicle should be as long as possible and is influenced by engine efficiency and also fuel capacity. Finally, cross-country mobility is dependent on track ground pressure, hull clearance, trench crossing and incline climbing capabilities and the ability to cross streams.

Armour protection is linked to the thickness and the quality of the steel-rolled plate and the angles applied to the superstructure and turret.

Above:
A group of tanks from 2.PzDiv take position on the outskirts of a village. Two PzKpfw IV and one PzKpfw III prepare to open fire on a distant target. During this phase of the war, the tanks of 2.PzDiv displayed a confusing variety of markings. (von Aufsess)

Below:
Forward elements of an
unknown *Panzerdivision*
come under a surprise
attack by conceal enemy
forces. A motorcycle
rider rushes away, as
the leading PzKPfw III
and a 2cm Flak SdKfz
10/4 cover the area,
ready to open fire. The
*Flak-Sturmgeschütz (Flak-
Sturm)* units were very
useful for providing quick,
accurate and hard hitting
fire support where it was
needed. (Anderson)

The level of protection has a direct effect on the proposed weight of a tank. While the French armaments industry preferred to manufacture hulls and turrets from cast steel, the Germans and the British preferred to fabricate them from rolled steel.

By 1940, the majority of the French tank force consisted of heavily armoured infantry tanks, and some 1,500 (R35) and 1,200 (H35/H39) were in service. Principally, both types were an improvement on the renowned Renault FT-17. Facing a modern German tank force, both types must be regarded as being inferior. The B1 medium tank was developed during the inter-war period. This 32-ton vehicle mounted a 4.7cm SA35 gun in a one-man turret and a 7.5cm ABS SA35 howitzer in the front of the hull. This tank had good armour protection, and was considered to be a dangerous opponent for the *Panzerwaffe* even when it was possible to be fired on by 8.8cm FlaK or heavy field artillery. On a single occasions, determined commitment by a B1 proved to be highly successful. The 10.PzDiv lost 13 PzKpfw III and IV to one skillfully deployed French B1 and after the battle the French tank returned home safe, its massive armour withstood all German shells. In 1940, more than 400 of the type were in French military service.

In 1936, the French introduced a new more modern combat tank, the Somua S35. This tank had the same turret as that used on the B1 and mounted the powerful 4.7cm SA35 gun. By May 1940, more than 400 of the type were issued to the *divisions légères mécaniques* (cavalry divisions).

In May 1940, the BEF was equipped with 300 tanks, and a further 300 had been delivered by 17 May. The majority of these were Vickers Mk VIB light tanks, which would prove to be unsuitable for the coming battle. A total of 73 machine-gun equipped A11 infantry tanks (with armour up to 80mm thick), were also available. The only type available to fight the German Panzer was the A13 Cruiser Tank (150 delivered) armed with an Ordnance QF (quick firing) 2-pounder gun which was certainly superior to the German 3.7cm gun. Also available were a very small number of A12 Infantry Tank Mk II (Matilda II) a well-armoured vehicle which mounted a QF 2-pounder gun.

Present-day historical research places great emphasis on the question; Why were the Germans able to defeat the Western Allies despite the alleged superiority in quality (and quantity) of the French and British tanks? Here the author must intervene. For the type warfare conducted by the German *Panzerwaffe*, the technical characteristics of the PzKpfw III

Above:
The 6.PzDiv had more than 110 PzKPfw 35(t) and 14 PzBefWg 35(t) command tanks. The meaning of the interlaced Z-symbols on the rear of the turrets is unknown. (Historyfacts)

Above:
A column of PzKpfw III tanks pass a horse-drawn supply column. The leading tank, an Ausf E, has some steel plates welded to the superstructure; possibly a repair of combat damage or perhaps the crew has increased the armour protection on the vehicle, against all regulations. (von Aufsess)

and IV were much better suited to battlefield conditions than those of French tanks.

In this context the simple comparison of only technical data is certainly not helpful. What did it matter whether the French S35 tank mounted a superior 4.7cm gun, if the commander had only barely sufficient observation means, and if he had to handle the gun alone thus reducing the rate of fire and neglecting his prime task?

Certainly it is true that both the S35 and the B1, and the British A12 Infantry Tank Mk II (Matilda) had armour protection impenetrable to the German 3.7cm tank gun. Indeed, the British A13 Cruiser Tank was similar in concept to a German tank. Both the A13 and the A12 had turrets manned by a crew of three. However, the A12 was available in very low numbers only, with only some 24 sent to the continent (also sent were some 70 of the seriously inferior A11 Matilda I).

After the attack, it became obvious that both the PzKpfw III and IV were suitable for upgrading in both terms of armour and armament: a great advantage in terms of production and supply.

French tanks were target-oriented designs, with small and somewhat cramped hulls manufactured from cast steel (with the exception of the B1). Any reinforcement of the armour protection or any up-gunning was impossible.

Existing British tanks were also not suited for upgrading with heavier armour or armament. However, this would not be necessary since a succeeding model, the Cruiser Mark VI was already in production. But, the British would have to wait until May 1942 for a more powerful tank gun, when the Ordnance QF 6-pounder gun replaced the 2 pounder.

Of far greater significance for the course of the invasion of France was seemingly another soft factor. In his book *L'Étrange Défaute* (*The Strange Defeat*) Marc Bloch, a French historian, wrote a remarkable assessment of some the facets of the German victory:

> The Germans waged a war of today, characterized by speed. We, on the other hand, did not only try and wage a war from yesterday…, we have also proven to be unable and unwilling to understand the rhythm of the new German strategy, which sounded the bell of a new era…
>
> … On all levels of the [German] military hierarchy; a certain willingness for expedient cooperation can be seen …

Below:
Three independent *Panzerjäger Abteilungen* were issued with armoured *mittlerer Zugkraftwagen* 8t (medium half-tracked tractor – SdKfz 7) towing an 8.8cm Flak 18. The task of these units was to destroy heavy French armour and they were used countless times to provide support for struggling infantry confronted by superior *Panzerfeind* (armoured enemy). (Münch)

Type Technical Data	PzKpfw III Ausf E	Somua S35	Cruiser Mk IVA (A13)
Armament	3.7cm L/45 Three MG 34	47mm L/32 One MG	40mm L/52 One MG
Crew	Five	Three	Three
Penetration at 100m	64mm	39mm	n/a
Penetration at 500m	31mm	33mm	50mm
Radio	yes	yes	yes
Armour, frontal	30mm	35 – 55mm	30mm
Weight	19.5t	20t	15t
Performance	265hp	190hp	340hp
Max speed	67kph	37kph	48kph
Power/weight ratio	13.6hp/t	9.5hp/t	22.7hp/t
Ground pressure	0.92kg/cm²	0.85kg/cm²	0.93kg/cm²
Cruising range, max	165km	260km	160km

Type Technical Data	PzKpfw IV Ausf D	Char B1	Infantry Tank Mk II (A12)
Armament	7.5cm L/24 Two MG 34	75mm L/17 47mm L/32 Two MG	40mm L/52 One MG
Crew	Five	Four	Four
Penetration at 100m	41mm	39mm (47mm gun)	n/a
Penetration at 500m	38mm	33mm (47mm gun)	50mm
Radio	yes	yes	yes
Armour, frontal	30mm	45 – 60mm	45 – 80mm
Weight	20t	32t	26t
Performance	265hp	300hp	2 x 94hp
Max speed	42kph	28kph	24kph
Power/weight ratio	13.2hp/t	9.4hp/t	7.2hp/t
Ground pressure	0.83kg/cm²	0.85kg/cm²	1.12kg/cm²
Cruising range, max	210km	140km	110km

Left:
An 8.8cm Flak 18 *auf Selbstfahrlafette Zugkraftwagen*, mounted on the chassis of a partly-armoured *schwerer Zugkraftwagen* 12t (heavy half-tracked tractor) SdKfz 8. The gun shield provided the crew with little protection against direct enemy fire, and left them very vulnerable to shell splinters. (Anderson)

During the entire campaign the Germans had a nasty habit: They emerged exactly there, where no one expected them to be. They simply did not comply with the rules…

His views are interesting, since the German citizen was indeed integrated into numerous organizations closely controlled by the state and the party, and sometimes even by his neighbours. In everyday life, any unwanted criticism or any opposition was futile and dangerous.

The German soldier, however, was led and inspired by *Auftragstaktik*, (mission-specific tactics). Marc Bloch (who died in 1944 fighting with the French Resistance) heavily criticized his own nation, which in the years before outbreak of war, was torn by inner conflicts between national and leftist political movements. He blamed especially the socialists and communists (the latter having been heavily influenced by the Soviet communist party) for their 'exaggerated pacifism'. France had proven to be unable to go to war…

Left:
An armoured SdKfz 7 towing an 8.8cm Flak 18 of sPzJgAbt 525. The combination did not prove to be successful in combat and was not deployed again after the French campaign. (Anderson)

Below:
A French B1 heavy tank and a Panhard P 178 armoured car lie abandoned at the roadside with a damaged PzKpfw 38(t). Many French types would be widely used later in the war as *Beutefahrzeuge* (captured vehicles). (Anderson)

Above:
A PzBefwg of 7.PzDiv rumbles down a wall and onto a beach for the benefit of propaganda photographers and film makers were certainly not far. The tank is fitted with the standard-type frame antenna. (NARA)

Above:
Erwin Rommel, the commander of 7.PzDiv, at a harbour in France with some miserable looking British officers captured at Dunkirk. (NARA)

Left:
Equipment abandoned by the British Expeditionary Force (BEF) and French forces, including a number of light carriers, litters the coast near Dunkirk. The vast number of soft-skinned vehicles captured in France, were put to good use by German forces. (Blancharde)

CHAPTER 9

BETWEEN THE CAMPAIGNS

Planning the invasion of Great Britain

After the invasion and occupation of the Netherlands, Belgium and France;, Adolf Hitler, although he appeared to want to avoid a war, was preparing a plan for a large-scale amphibious landing on the south coast of Britain. In November 1939, the *Organisationsabteilung* prepared the 'Nordwest' study:

> The honourable Chief of the General Staff decided to examine the possibility of a landing in England. We are proposing a large-scale airborne landing, possibly assisted by Italian air transport capacity, in close cooperation with army troops. The occupation of the Dutch-Belgian coast is prerequisite, since it will be used as starting position for sea and air transports... The North Sea has to be cleared of all British naval forces... The study is code named '*Nordwest*'. The following considerations have to be explored:

- Possibilities for transferring large parts of both army and *Luftwaffe* over the channel...

Estimated requirements of forces:

- One army headquarters
- Three corps headquarters
- Two *Panzerdivisionen*
- Four Infantry divisions

Left:
A *Tauchpanzer* of 3.Kp *Tauchpanzer-Abteilung* during trials at the Werbellinsee, north of Berlin shortly before the launch of *Unternehmen* (Operation) *Barbarossa*. Everything except the commander's cupola cover have been sealed. (Anderson)

- One Infantry division (motorized)
- Seven *Fliegerdivisions*
- 16 *Luftlande* IR
- Further army troops…

In August 1940, the commander-in-chief of the army issued this order:

Instructions for preparation of *Unternehmen Seelöwe*

Mission:

The *Oberbefehlshaber* has instructed the army to prepare for an assault landing on the coast of England. Purpose of this attack is to disable the British motherland as a base for the continuation of the war against Germany. If necessary, the country has to be totally occupied. The order for the execution depends on the political situation. The preparations must be taken in a way that the execution can start on 15 September…

The operation is code named *Seelöwe*.

For *Unternehmen Seelöwe* (Operation *Sealion*) absolute superiority in the air

Below:
So confident was the German hierarchy that Britain would be conquered they had this leaflet written and printed for distribution to the population. (Anderson)

Geheime Kommandofache

Aufruf
an die Bevölkerung Englands.

§ 1.

Das von den deutschen Truppen besetzte englische Gebiet wird unter deutsche Militärverwaltung gestellt.

§ 2.

Die militärischen Befehlshaber werden die zur Sicherung der Truppe und zur Aufrechterhaltung der allgemeinen Sicherheit und Ordnung nötigen Anordnungen erlassen.

§ 3.

Die Truppen werden, wenn die Bevölkerung sich ordnungsgemäß verhält, Personen und Eigentum schonen.

§ 4.

Die Landesbehörden dürfen, wenn sie sich loyal verhalten, weiterarbeiten.

§ 5.

Alle unbesonnenen Handlungen, jede Art von Sabotage, passiver oder aktiver Widerstand gegen die deutsche Wehrmacht haben schärfste Vergeltungsmaßnahmen zur Folge.

§ 6.

Ich warne alle Zivilpersonen vor Kampfhandlungen gegen die deutsche Truppe. Sie werden unnachsichtlich mit dem Tode bestraft.

§ 7.

Den Anordnungen der deutschen Militärbehörden ist Folge zu leisten. Ungehorsam wird schärfstens bestraft.

Der Oberbefehlshaber des Heeres.

Appeal
to the population of England.

§ 1.

English territory occupied by the German Armed Forces will be placed under German Military Administration.

§ 2.

The military Commanders will take all necessary steps to ensure the security of the Armed Forces and for the maintenance of public order and security.

§ 3.

Provided that the population behaves in an orderly manner, the Armed Forces will respect person and property.

§ 4.

Provided that they maintain an honourable attitude, the local authorities will be allowed to continue to function.

§ 5.

Any ill-considered act, any form of sabotage, any resistance, active or passive, against the German Armed Forces, will be met with the sharpest possible reprisals.

§ 6.

I hereby warn all civilians against the commitment of any hostile acts against the German Armed Forces. Such acts will be remorselessly punished by sentence of death.

§ 7.

The Orders of the German Military Authorities are to be obeyed. Disobedience will be severely punished.

The Commander-in-Chief of the Army.

and at sea was imperative. The OKW assumed that after eliminating the Royal Navy and the Royal Air Force, all British resistance would collapse and the country would seek to negotiate a peace treaty.

However, the *Kriegsmarine* (German Navy) under Admiral Raeder opposed *Seelöwe* after taking a more realistic view of the actual facts. At the conclusion of *Weserübung* [Norway campaign], the German fleet was hopelessly outnumbered by the Royal Navy. In a joint analysis, both the *Kriegsmarine* and the *Luftwaffe* demanded that priority must be given to the total destruction the Royal Air Force. This formidable task was the sole responsibility of the *Luftwaffe* and its commander-in-chief, *Generalfeldmarschall* Göring.

While the *Luftwaffe* fought in the skies, Hitler issued orders for the preparation of the invasion. A fleet of 155 transport ships, 2,000 landing vessels was assembled, but only some 500 were specialized *Marinefährprahm* (tactical landing craft). A large number were commandeered river cargo barges, many of which were modified by removing the bow and a door fitted. Unloading ramps were carried inside the vessel.

In the summer of 1940, German army units stationed in the occupied west practised loading and unloading equipment. *Trockenrampen* (land-based loading ramps), were constructed to train vehicle drivers on how to enter and leave a barge under difficult conditions.

The most dangerous and decisive phase of the landing would be the unloading, as the mobility of soft-skinned and armoured vehicles would be seriously hampered in the wet sand. Specialized pioneer equipment necessary for the operation could not be produced due to the short time period (and a lack of resources) before the landing. For this reason many different

Above:
Germany did not have the military means to undertake an amphibious invasion, or the facilities for production of special vessels. The *Siebelfähre* (Siebel ferry), named after its inventor, was assembled by using available pontoons; a versatile but makeshift solution. Heavily-armed *Kampffähren* (combat ferries) carried various weapons, such as this *Flakfähre* carrying four 8.8cm Flak guns. (Späten)

Above:
Unloading exercises for the invasion: a *Sturmgeschütz* (StuG), laden with infantrymen, leaves down a ramp from a modified river barge. The bow section of the vessel would have been blown off by explosive charges. (Anderson)

makeshift solutions were developed by the troops from their own resources. Special vehicle tracks made of corrugated sheeting or heavy wooden boards would be used to assist the vehicles to leave the beach rapidly. Fascine bundles were to be carried on the vehicles. At that time no specialized armoured vehicle had been designed to support a landing.

Tauchpanzer – Submersible tanks

The tank was progressively developed and modified to improve mobility and to extend its range of applications. In the 1920s, the first amphibious and submersible tanks were developed and tested. Without doubt, the Soviet Union was at the forefront of development and built a total of 4,000 amphibious versions of their T-37, T-38 and T-40 tanks.

For the proposed *Unternehmen Seelöwe* landing, specialized armoured vehicles were required – tanks ready to enter combat from the moment of reaching the beach. Possible solutions ranged from swimming to fully-submersible vehicles, and all German tanks then in production proved to be suitable for conversion. The PzKpfw II was fitted with two (one each side) simple pontoons, *Auftriebskörper* (floats), which allowed the tank to travel at 10kph through a moderate seaway with its armament ready to fire. Some 52 vehicles were available by the summer of 1940.

For the heavier PzKpfw III and IV production of swimming devices was not possible. Due to the lack of time, the *Heereswaffenamt* decided on a conversion kit for a fully-submersible tank. The technical implementation would be difficult, but feasible and due to the relative similarity of both designs the modifications would be similar. All converted PzKpfw III and IV received the suffix (T) for *Tauchfähig* (submersible).

A list detailing the necessary modifications dated 14 August 1940:

- The maintenance and signal hatches on the hull, superstructure and turret were provided with extra rubber seals. All direct holes in the armour for cables or any attachments were closed. Hinges and screws were covered with a sealing compound. The gaps around the engine, transmission or brake access hatches were additionally sealed by tarred-paper tape.

Below:
An operational *Tauchpanzer* III ready for deployment; all apertures have been sealed, a 15m long large-bore hose, attached to a float, supplied breathing air for the crew and combustion air for the engine. (Anderson)

- The final drives and the bearings of the running gear components were sealed by fabric soaked with 'Teroson'.
- The driver's visor was covered by a sheet-metal plate, the ball mount of the bow MG 34 by a rubber hood. Vision was provided by glass windows.
- The cooling-air inlets and outlets were covered by sheet-metal plates. The cooling system was converted to use sea water. Inflow and outflow was provided through a valve located in the left cooling-air inlet.
- The normal exhaust mufflers were removed and substituted by non-return valves.
- The turret ring was sealed by a rubber gland, inflated from the inside. A protective flange was welded around the base of the turret.
- A metal frame was welded to the front plate of the turret. The complete gun mantlet including the co-axially mounted MG 34 was protected by a rubber cover, sealed by a band clamp. Vision for the optics was provided by windows made from 'Zellon', a transparent synthetic material.
- The commander's cupola was covered by a rubber hood.
- Breathing air for the crew and combustion air for the engine was provided by a 15m long and 110mm diameter reinforced hose, which was attached to the rubber hood over the cupola. The hose was mounted to a float fabricated from balsa wood.

Below:
Men of StuG Abt 184 use a *Trockenrampe* as they practice for embarkation onto river barges. The Maybach Variorex gearbox fitted in the PzKpfw III Ausf E and F, also the StuG Ausf A proved to be difficult to operate, making smooth starting and stopping difficult. (Anderson)

- The driver and the gunner had a depth gauge, and a steering compass was used for navigation. Radio communication was ensured by an antenna mounted on top of the buoy.
- A bilge pump was fitted to clear water out of the vehicle.

It is obvious that some of the final exterior waterproofing would be completed by a service crew after the tank crew was inside the vehicle. All these modifications were for one mission only.

It was planned to transport the *Tauchpanzer* on railway ferries, as up to 40 tanks could be carried on each vessel. On reaching the enemy coast, the tanks would be unloaded down a bow ramp in shallow water, or lowered by crane if the water was up to 10m deep. After reaching the beach, the gun and secondary armament could be brought into action without removing the sealing covers. The rubber hood over the commander's cupola was blown off by a small explosive charge, and the sealing gland for the turret ring was deflated to enable the turret to rotate.

The *Schwimmpanzer* II and the *Tauchpanzer* III and IV were allotted to four units: *Tauchpanzer Abteilungen* A, B, C, and D. All the units were organized according to the *leichte Panzerkompanie* (b) KStN 1171 (*Behelfs*)

Above:
In preparation for the invasion the river barges were modified by cutting off the shaped bow section and replacing this with a flat loading door. A loading ramp was carried in the cargo space. (Späten)

Right:
During preparations for *Unternehmen Seelöwe*. (Operation Sealion) some 1,300 river barges were commandeered by the Germans and positioned in Dutch, Belgian and French ports along the occupied Channel coast. (Späten)

dated July 1940, which had a mixed establishment of tanks. By August 1940, 152 *Tauchpanzer* III, 48 *Tauchpanzer* IV and 52 *Schwimmpanzer* II were reported as being operational.

During the course of these preparations, Hitler still hoped that Churchill would agree to a peace treaty and ordered secret negotiations with the British government to be opened in Sweden. Although the talks failed, Hitler decided to postpone *Unternehmen Seelöwe* in October 1940, but gave orders to continue the preparations for an invasion in the spring 1941. However, after his decision to invade Soviet Russia on 22 June 1941, *Unternehmen Seelöwe* was consigned to history.

The conversion of PzKpfw III and IV to *Tauchpanzer* standard continued until early 1941.

Below:
A StuG of StuGAbt 184 is carefully reversed into the cargo space of a river barge during an exercise. (Anderson)

Above:
A PzKpfw II fitted with *Schwimmkörper* on board of a train ferry. When the coast was reached, the tank would leave the ship and 'swim' to the beach where the floats would be detached. (Historyfacts).

Right:
The *Marinefährprahm* (MFP) was a specialized and sophisticated landing vessel available in different versions. By late 1940, two types were available, the *Typ* (Type) A had a capacity of 100 tons, and the *Typ* B carried 140 tons. (Späten)

The state of the *Panzerwaffe*

An expansion of the *Panzerwaffe* was important to Hitler and his ambitions. The invasion of France was to be accomplished by deploying ten *Panzerdivisionen*, each had two tank regiments with a complement of some 250 tanks. In May 1940, around 60 percent of these were PzKpfw I and II.

However, before *Fall Gelb* (Plan Yellow) it had already been decided to increase the fighting power of the *Panzerdivisionen*. Of prime importance was the upgrading of the main combat tank, the PzKpfw III by mounting a 5cm gun; an improvement to frontal armour on the type was regarded as being of equal importance.

In July 1940, production of the PzKpfw III mounting the 5cm KwK L/42 began and by December that year 466 had been built. In September 1940, a large number of 'older' *Ausführungen* (production versions) underwent a modification programme:

Above:
Starting late 1940, many PzKpfw III Ausf E, F, and G were up-gunned by installing the 5cm KwK L/42. At the same time, additional 30mm armour plates were bolted to the bow, the plate protecting the driver and machine-gunner and also to rear of the hull. This particular vehicle is an upgraded Ausf G fitted with 40cm tracks. (Anderson)

- Remove the 3.7cm gun and replace with the 5cm KwK L/42.
- Fit 30mm add-on armour to the hull and superstructure front.
- Fit wider (40cm) tracks.

At the same time, the PzKpfw IV was also being improved by adding 30mm armour plates.

In 1940, the PzKpfw 35(t) and 38(t) were used as a substitute for the 3.7cm armed PzKpfw III. By that time, production of the PzKpfw 35(t) had ended, but some 160 remained in service with PzRgt 11. The PzKpfw 38(t), was certainly a better design and remained in production until mid-1942. Over 1,400 were built.

These Czech-built tanks performed a vital role in the early success of the *Panzerwaffe*.

Expanding the *Panzerdivisionen*

Directly after the Western campaign, the OKH implemented their far reaching plans to improve the attacking might of the German army. Over a

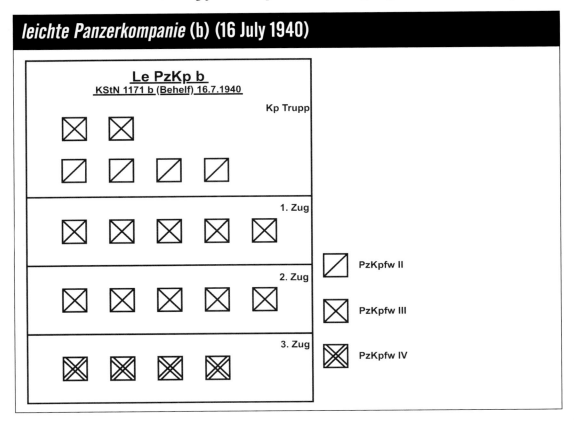

leichte Panzerkompanie (b) (16 July 1940)

period of six months, the number of *Panzerdivisionen* was doubled. In this miraculous multiplication, two of the four battalions in 1.PzDiv to 5.PzDiv were released to create new units and a further five *Panzerdivisionen* were newly established.

Thus the number of tanks in each division was reduced significantly, to an average of 150. How could this improve the attacking might?

The *Kriegsstärkenachweisung* (KStN – tables of organization) were adapted to the new requirements. In July 1940, a new structure was published, the *leichte Panzerkompanie* (b) KStN 1171 (*Behelfs*). This official structure shows a mixed establishment equipped with PzKpfw III and IV. The suffix *Behelfs* (makeshift) proves that this was not a standard structure, but a special one to be applied in specific tactical situations. *Panzer* companies used in isolated commitments (as anticipated with the proposed landing in Britain) would benefit from having escort tanks available. However, the actual allocation of tanks was the responsibility of

Below:
A PzKpfw IV Ausf E the hull of which has improved amour protection of 50mm. However, the plate in front of the driver was still 30mm thick, so brackets were welded on to allow the attachment of an additional 30mm of armour. A shortage of material resulted in insufficient delivery of such plates, and this resulted in different levels of protection on production tanks. (Anderson)

Right:
This PzKpfw IV Ausf C is fitted with an extra 20mm armour plate bolted to the front of the hull, increasing this to 50mm. The majority of these early vehicles remained in service with *Panzerersatz-und-Ausbildungsabteilungen* (tank replacement and training battalions). (Anderson)

the battalion commander. He could easily order single PzKpfw IV, or a platoon to reinforce the light companies.

In February 1941, both the *leichte* and *mittlere Panzerkompanie* were reorganized. This was possible because of the growing number of available combat tanks (PzKpfw III and IV). The light company now had an authorized strength of 17 PzKpfw III, the medium company had 14 PzKpfw IV, reaching the OKW's planned complement as announced by Fritsch in 1936. However, it must be clear that these numbers were of a pure academic nature, and in reality, this target was normally not reached. Combat losses also affected this preferred figure.

Virtually all PzKpfw I light tanks were withdrawn from all front-line units. Considerable numbers were allocated to the *Panzerpionierkompanie* (PzPiKp – armoured engineer companies) of the *Panzerdivsion*, and many of these vehicles were converted to *Ladungsleger* (explosive charge carrier) or bridging section carriers.

Also large numbers were allocated to replacement and training battalions, while others were rebuilt as specialized vehicles including ammunition and supply carriers.

leichte Panzerkompanie (1 February 1941)

Leichte PzKp
KStN 1171 (Sd) 1.2.1941
Kp Trupp
1. Zug
2. Zug
3. Zug

☐ PzKpfw II

☒ PzKpfw III

Mittlerer Panzerkompanie (1 February 1941)

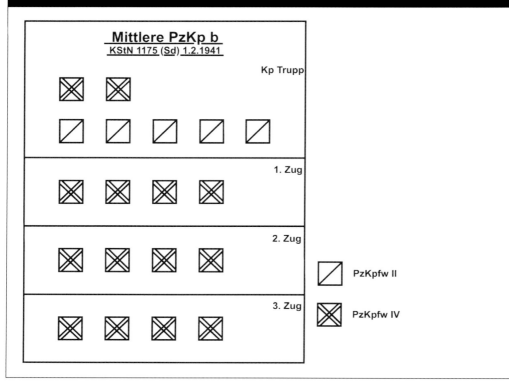

CHAPTER 10

SONNENBLUME — A WAR OF LOGISTICS?

After the successful campaign against the Low Countries and France, also the peace pact with Soviet Russia, Hitler felt that he was in a secure position. However, Britan remained a problem in his drive to control Europe and he began planning an invasion, *Unternehmen Seelöwe*. To assist with this plan, German officials attempted to persuade their allies to enter the war. Spain appeared interested, but claimed to lack the necessary military equipment and also made unacceptable territorial demands.

Italy, ruled by the fascist dictator Benito Mussolini, was approached. The country had already declared war on Britain and France on 10 June 1940. For the proposed invasion, Hitler wanted a second front to tie-down large parts of the British forces, and the fragile situation in North Africa appeared to fit this plan. It is not known as to how far the German initiative influenced the Italians, but on 9 September Mussolini ordered an offensive to be launched against British forces stationed in Egypt. The vital Suez Canal was threatened.

The Italian commander-in-chief, *Maresciallo d'Italia* Rodolfo Graziani was unwilling, as he was certain that his forces were too weak, but nevertheless he obeyed the order. The Italian army of the day was equipped and organized to fight a colonial war, and mainly consisted of infantry forces with very limited mechanized equipment. The Italian X Corps proved to be ill-equipped to conduct a modern mobile war under the difficult conditions of the North African desert. The following offensive brought only small territorial gains, as the numerically inferior British forces decided to avoid battle. By mid-September, the Italian assault came to a stalemate. In this dangerous situation Italian forces had lost the initiative, and urgently requested reinforcements

Left:
Erwin Rommel with General Ludwig Crüwell, commanding officer of the *Deutsches Afrika Korps* (DAK), who was vehemently opposed to Rommel's decision to launch a counterattack against British forces on November 1941. Rommel used an SdKfz 250/3 (the command version of the armoured light halftrack) to travel around the battlefield. (Hansen)

Above:
The crew of a Semovente da 75/18 M40 *Comando*, have set up an artillery observation and range-finding post on top of the vehicle. (Anderson)

Right:
By 1941, the Carro Armato M11/39 medium tank was the mainstay of the Italian forces on the North African battlefield. It mounted a 37mm Vickers-Terni L/42 gun in the hull (with limited traverse), and two 8mm Breda 38 machine guns in a small turret. The gun was clearly out-classed by the British Ordnance QF 2-pounder gun mounted in cruiser and infantry tanks. (Guglielmi)

did not arrive. The British, however, were able to send reinforcements. On 8 December, a counterattack was launched, called Operation *Compass*. British and Commonwealth troops equipped with the Infantry Tank Mk II Matilda II and Cruiser Tanks, proved to be far superior and the tank units attached to the Italian X Corps were almost annihilated. Exploiting this success the British continued their advance. Within ten weeks of fighting, the British forces advanced some 1,500km into Libya taking the cities of Sollum, Bardia and Tobruk, and at the same time captured vast stocks of Italian equipment.

Facing this development, German officials decided to send military forces to relieve the Italian army. The British advance was to be stopped and thrown back.

On 11 January 1940, the *Führerhauptquartier* published *Weisung* Nr. 22. This directive from the *Führer* set clear targets:

FHQu, den 11.1.41
Der Führer und Oberste Befehlshaber der Wehrmacht
OKW/WFSt/Abt. L Nr. 44018/41 g.K. Chefs.

Geheime-Kommandosache
Chef Sache
Nur durch Offizier

Weisung Nr. 22

Aid of German forces fighting in the Mediterranean
The situation in the Mediterranean region, where Britain has committed superior forces against our Allies, requires German assistance for strategic, political and psychological reasons.
Tripolitania must be held, and the danger of a collapse of the Albanian front eliminated. Furthermore, the Italian army group *Cavallero* must be empowered to start an offensive in Albania in connection with [our] later operations.
For these reasons I order:
1. A force will be established by the Commander-in-Chief, which will assist our Allies defending Tripolitania, especially against the British tank divisions. The basic requirements of its structure will be ordered separately.
The preparations are to be planned in such a way, that this force will be transferred to Tripoli following the transportation of one Italian tank and one motorized division (estimated from 20 February)...
2. The X.Fl Korps will maintain Sicily as its base of operations. Its most important task is to combat British naval forces and sea transport between the western and eastern parts of the Mediterranean...

Adolf Hitler

Rommel in Africa

For the German leadership, the decision to send military forces to assist Italy in removing British forces from Egypt was not an easy one, as Hitler had already made his decision to invade Soviet Russia. For this simple, but decisive reason, the supreme command of the army could neither afford to send large-scale formations nor provide the necessary long-term supply.

In late 1940, General Ritter von Thoma had been sent to Libya to evaluate the situation. His report came to the following conclusion:

> The decisive factor will be the supply problem. This not only because of the climatic and terrain difficulties in the desert, but because of the British navys' command of the Mediterranean. It will be extremely difficult, if not impossible to supply and maintain a large army. If Germany does send a force to support the Italians, it should be an armoured force and at least four armoured divisions would be necessary to ensure success…. This is also the maximum force that could be effectively maintained with supplies…

On 8 March 1941, PzRgt 5, formerly part of the 3.PzDiv, was sent to Tripoli. During loading in Naples, there was a fire onboard one of the transport ships and 13 combat tanks were lost. The unit arrived with 25 PzKpfw I, 45 PzKpfw II, 71 PzKpfw III (5cm L/42), 20 PzKpfw IV and seven command tanks. Immediately after unloading in Tripoli, PzRgt 5 paraded through the city in a show of force.

Another more subtle signal was the appointment of *Generalleutnant* Erwin Rommel as the commander of the force. Rommel was certainly a protagonist of modern mobile warfare. The speed at which the 7.PzDiv advanced through France even surprised military leaders in Berlin. Rommel fully-appreciated the capabilities of the tank and how to deploy his force as the battle developed. Almost equally important, was his ability to lead his force of determined and highly-trained soldiers and was always to be seen as near to the battlefront as was safely possible. The author has interviewed a number of *Afrikakorps* veterans, and all stated that they would have gone through hell for Rommel.

According to orders, the German detachment was to create a buffer-zone that was intended to stop the British tank forces advancing further west: but Rommel thought otherwise.

In mid-March, Rommel returned to Berlin and presented his plans to his superiors. His request for more forces was denied. *Generaloberst* Franz Halder, the chief of the OKH General Staff, wrote in his diary:

> Even if we had two further *Panzerkorps* available, how would you supply and feed them. Rommel replied sarcastically: ('I don't care, that is your business')

Below:
A PzKpfw III Ausf G or H being loaded onto a transport ship; A *Gepäckkasten* (stowage bin, sometimes referred to as a *Rommelkiste*) has been fitted to the rear of the turret. The vehicle is fitted with the 36cm track, but the last road wheel is of the later, wider type, designed for the 40cm track. (Anderson)

Above:
Men of PzRgt 8 gather in the morning cold. A PzBefWg of the staff section, the vehicle had a frame antenna mounted on the rear and both radio aerials have been raised. These command tanks were not armed, but were fitted with a dummy main gun. The tank had only one ball-mounted machine gun fitted in the mantlet. (Anderson)

Rommel knew the British. His PzRgt 5 had more than 70 of the latest PzKpfw III, mounting a 5cm KwK L/42 and 20 PzKpfw IV tanks. Virtually all were fitted with improved frontal armour to provide protection against fire from the British 40mm Ordnance QF (quick firing) 2-pounder, a potent anti-tank (AT) gun.

The British knew Rommel and decided to retreat carefully, as positions in the far west would be difficult to hold and keep supplied. The retreat was called Operation *Laxative*, a true example of British military humour describing a smooth exit.

At that time, the Cruiser Tank Mk IVA (A13, Mk II) was the main British battle tank. By mid-1941, it was superseded by the Mk VI (A15) Crusader I but, as no better gun was available it mounted the QF 2-pounder that only fired armour-piercing (AP) rounds. The same gun was mounted in the Infantry Tank Mk II (A12) Matilda II which was built with very strong armour. However, mechanized warfare in the desert required speed and manoeuvrability and was not suitable for slow moving infantry tanks.

On 31 March, PzRgt 5 advanced to Marsa al-Brega which was to be the starting point for the action to regain Cyrenaica. Unlike the commanders of Italian mechanized forces, who preferred to advance their forces along the paved coastal roads, Rommel preferred to split his forces and use the roads or the desert. On 4 April, when Benghazi was taken a southern battle group, containing a large part of PzRgt 5, had moved directly through the desert.

The first battle at Marsa al-Brega was a short, but fierce one in which six British Crusader tanks were lost while PzRgt 5 lost two PzKpw III and a PzKpfw IV. During the coming days German forces, as always supported by Italian troops, extended their probing attacks to an all-out offensive intended to sweep British forces out of Cyrenaica. Rommel achieved this with only 50 percent of his forces (the 15.PzDiv had not arrived) in just 12 days and his stunning success not only impressed the German supreme command, but also his British foe. However, Rommel had ignored his orders from Berlin.

His forces continued to advance through the desert and finally reached the Egyptian border and the city of Tobruk, where British and Australian troops were trapped and besieged for 33 weeks.

Unhappy with Rommel's actions *Generaloberst* Halder sent his deputy, General von Paulus (not the later commander of the 6.Army), to find out why he had ignored his orders. At the time Rommel was unaware of the forthcoming *Unternehmen Barbarossa*. It is possible that Rommel was influenced by this rebuke, also at that time his troops began to feel the effects of the overextended supply lines. Fuel, ammunition, water and all other essential supplies had to be transported from the ports of Tripoli and Benghazi: a distance of 1,500km. It is obvious that a large proportion of valuable fuel was being consumed by the transport vehicles of the supply columns.

Above:
A PzKpfw III Ausf G or H with fuel cans stowed on top of the turret, and water cans on the track cover, indispensable items for during the long marches in the desert. The ubiquitous black palm-tree emblem of the *Afrika Korps* is painted next to the driver's vision visor. (Zimmermann)

Above::
A 5cm KwK L/42 armed
PzKpfw III Ausf J of 7.Kp,
PzRgt 8, 15.PzDiv, has
been barely camouflaged
with desert brush while
undergoing routine
maintenance work. The
7.Kp identifier is visible
on the side of the turret.
(NARA)

Furthermore, the rapid advance revealed many serious technical problems suffered by German tanks. From an after action report by PzRgt 5 dated May 1941:

The average range of more than 700km covered had negative effects on the tanks. Until the moment the regiment took up positions at Tobruk, a large numbers of tanks had to be sent to the workshop company:

12 out of 25 Pzkpfw I
Two out of three kl PzBefWg (command tank)
19 out of 45 PzKpfw II
44 out of 65 PzKpfw III and PzBefWg III
Six out of 17 PzKpfw IV

The reason for the breakdowns was the crossing of the desert near Fort el Abd at a very high speed, which was necessary tactical requirements. A total of 65 PzKpfw III and 44 grPzBefWg failed due to severe engine problems… Reason was in all cases the very fine dust which formed a thick paste which clogged the crankcase. The workshop company had to exchange 58 engines… The available air filters are absolutely unsuited for desert use, since they do not prevent the fine dust… We suggest utilization of dry felt filters as used on British cars, trucks and tanks…

These problems originated from the hasty deployment of German forces in desert conditions. However, technical matters can be solved, and better air filters were soon available.

Between April and May 1941, the *Deutsches Afrikakorps* was reinforced by a second unit, the 15.PzDiv whose PzRgt 8 had a complement of 45 PzKpfw II, 71 PzKPfw III, 20 PzKpfw IV and ten command tanks.

On 15 May, British forces launched Operation *Brevity* the main objective of which was to break the siege of Tobruk. German supply lines were constantly under threat of attack from Australian and British forces, which required Rommel to maintain a substantial tank force around the city. Subsequently, the border area of Egypt was held by a relatively small German force. The British launched an infantry assault supported by 24 Matilda II tanks, with the flanks of the attack protected by Cruiser Tank Mk IV and Mk VI tanks. The heavily armoured Matilda II proved to be immune to fire from the 5cm KwK L/42 armed PzKpfw III and even the 7.5cm KwK L/24 armed PzKpfw IV: only a lucky shot on a track or the turret ring was able to stop this tank. In some instances, the impact of a 7.5cm high-explosive (HE) shell could cause the turret traversing mechanism to lock. However, the British QF 2-pounder gun, reduced their fighting ability as the gun fired only AP shells and not an HE round suitable against soft targets.

The British Infantry Tank Mk II (A12) Matilda II was a unique design which had all-around armour protection of 60 to 80mm and proved to be

Below:
A British Cruiser Tank Mk IV A (A13 Mk II) carrying the name 'Encounter' appears to have been captured intact. This improved Mk IV A was a fast and manoeuvrable vehicle which had 30mm armour at the front. (Anderson)

Left:
A 5cm-armed PzKpfw III
Ausf G or H with a rack
(possibly an 'in the field'
modification) mounted
on the rear of the engine
compartment to allow
more supplies and spare
parts to be carried. (Getty)

Above::
Towed by the ubiquitous
s ZgKw 8t, a section
of 8.8cm Flak 18 guns
arrive in support of the
advance by PzRgt 8. In
an emergency these
guns would be instantly
unlimbered and cleared
for action. Fire from the
Flak 18 was very effective
against the heavily
armoured Matilda II even
at long range. (Anderson)

immune to all German tank guns. This forced Rommel to support his tank assaults with heavy guns: the fearsome 8.8cm anti-aircraft (AA) *Flugzeugabwehrkanone* (Flak) in *Panzerbegleitbatterien* (tank escort batteries) towed by half-tracked prime movers. One unit, Flak Regiment 33 had great success in many dangerous commitments; their long-range guns being decisively used to support the flanks during advances by German Panzers.

To bolster their forces the Germans were always looking to capture British equipment, in particular the Matilda II. One *Feldwebel* Peter Scherzberg, wrote a personal report which he wanted to be published in German newspapers explaining his experiences during Operation *Brevity*. The article was never published for reasons of secrecy:

Alert on the Sollum front as the British attempt to break through the German lines. In several waves the Matilda II tanks attacked our positions. The enemy deployed great numbers to reach his target, Bardia and two days later Tobruk. They relied on their Matilda II. This tank was said to be unbeatable, its strong armour made it untouchable...

German tank units were thrown against the Tommy [British forces], the greatest tank battle in Africa, if not in the world, evolved... By the third day the Tommy lost his confidence, his attack failed...

In the late afternoon, two men were sent out to recover a Matilda II which had failed at the barbed-wire defences separating Egypt from Libya... Upon reaching the tank, the men climbed in. It was indeed intact. The fuel tanks were full, the engine was started [the Matilda II had two engines.

Below:
An '*Acht-Acht*' (Eight-Eight) fires at a selected target. The FlaK 18 fired effective high-explosive (HE) and armour-piercing (AP) rounds, making it the ideal dual-purpose gun. However, the crew was always exposed to return fire from enemy weapons. (NARA)

A Swastika flag raised, and it was returned to cheers from our comrades back to our lines…

The next day, when the British were finally repulsed, after enormous human and material loss, further recovery troops were sent out… Only a few days later nine Matilda IIs moved east to fight against their former owners…

Operation *Brevity* forced Rommel to launch counterattacks. From an after action report by PzRgt 5 dated 15 May:

> I report on an attack by British Matilda II tanks. Our unit obtained support of 8.8cm Flak at Fort Capuzzo. We started a fierce battle with 16 Matilda IIs… Due to the limited effect of our weapons we could not stop the enemy or make him change his line of attack… I had too few tanks available to deploy, the only way to attack the Mk II tanks is with the combined fire from several 5cm tank guns at close range. We tried to turn off, a difficult manoeuvre during the fierce tank battle…
>
> At 08.25hrs, the 12 remaining tanks of *Panzerabteilung* Hohmann have the next encounter with the Matilda II tanks… We slowly retreat to Fort Capuzzo… At 08.40hrs, I report that Fort Capuzzo is in the hands of the enemy and we had to retreat as we had run out of ammunition. At 08.50hrs, I retreat with ten combat ready ranks to positions 5 to 6km north of Fort Capuzzo to be replenished with ammunition…

The initial impetus of Operation *Brevity* was quickly lost, by mid-May the British had retreated to the Halfaya Pass. Some ten days later, Rommel's next offensive *Unternehmen Skorpion* (Operation Scorpion) brought this important supply route back under German control again.

In mid-June, the British launched Operation *Battleaxe*, when they attacked the Pass of Halfaya in another attempt to relieve Tobruk. In a great westbound movement, Sollum was taken. While these attacks were repulsed by relatively weak German forces, the main part of PzRgt 5 moved south through the desert to strike both at the western flank and the rear of the British force. Operation *Battleaxe* had to be stopped. Axis forces had stabilized the Sollum front and the siege of Tobruk continued. According to German reports, the *Afrikakorps* lost some 25 tanks but more than 150 enemy tanks were destroyed.

After Operation *Battleaxe*, both sides were exhausted. Rommel had deliberately and somewhat carelessly over-extended his lines of supply and by mid-1941, the situation became critical.

On 1 August 1941, the 5.le Division was reorganized as 21.*Panzerdivision*.

British and Commonwealth forces, now known as the Eighth Army, were again quicker to recover and on 19 November 1941, launched Operation *Crusader*. The *Afrikakorps* joined the battle and attacked the British wherever possible. In November, the 4th Armoured Brigade was attacked. From an after action report by PzRgt 8 dated 22 November 1941:

Left:
The slow but heavily armoured and well-armed British Infantry Tank A12 Mk II (Matilda II) was highly prized by the Germans. A number of these tanks were captured during 1941, and subsequently used against British forces in a number of actions. The Germans clearly marked their *Beutepanzer* to avoid attack by their own forces. (Anderson)

At 14.00hrs on 22 November 1941, PzRgt 8, assisted by I. and III.Art Rgt 33 and III.FlaKRgt 33 advanced west along the Djebel south of Fort Capuzzo and attacked a strong enemy group near Sidi Muftah… The regiment moves at high speed to get to the enemy before nightfall… At 16.15hrs, the light platoon reports dark shapes dead ahead. The regiment advances at high speed in westerly direction, dazzled by the setting sun, and finally turns northwest in order to attack. Immediately, I. *Abteilung* attacks with great speed, while II. *Abteilung* follows positioned slightly to the right. The enemy opens fire from long range (2,000 to 3,000m). The regiment knocks-out all enemy tanks, despite stiff resistance. The enemy's supply column hastily withdraws in a northwest and north-east direction. Now the enemy attempts to counterattack the regiment with new tanks. The regimental commander orders the II. *Abteilung*, by radio, to transfer from the right to the left flank. Despite the high speed, the companies perform this manoeuvre successfully…

The regiment fights until sunset, and destroys numerous enemy tanks and some self-propelled anti-tank (SP AT) guns. The main part of the enemy force, however, used the cover of the night to retreat to Point 175…

At 18.45hrs, I. *Abteilung* unexpectedly meets a large group of enemy tanks packed tightly together. Due to complete darkness they are only recognizable at a very short distance of 10 to 20m. Friend and foe are stunned, no round is fired. Major Fenski, commander of I.*Abteilung*, realizes the situation first and crosses the hostile position in his *Befehlswagen*, and orders 1.*Kompanie* to encircle the enemy to the left, and 2.*Kompanie* do the same to the right.

Type Technical Data	PzKpfw III Ausf G verstärkt	Cruiser Mk VI (A15) Crusader I	PzKpfw IV Ausf E	Infantry Tank Mk II (A12) Matilda II
Armament	5cm L/42 Two MG 34	2-pdr QF Two .303in MG	7.5cm L/24 Two MG 34	40 mm L/52 One.303in MG
Crew	Five	Five	Five	Four
Penetration at 100m	94mm	n/a	41mm	n/a
Penetration at 500m	55mm	50mm	38mm	50mm
Radio	yes	yes	yes	yes
Armour, frontal	30 + 30mm	40mm	30 + 30mm	45 – 80mm
Weight	19.5t	18t	20t	26t
Performance	265hp	340hp	265hp	2 x 94hp
Max speed	67kph	44kph	42kph	24kph
Power/weight ratio	13.6hp/t	18.8hp/t	13.2hp/t	7.2hp/t
Ground pressure	0.92kg/cm²	1.04kg/cm²	0.83kg/cm²	1.12kg/cm²
Cruising range, max	165km	210km	210km	110km

Oberleutnant Bock, the adjutant, fires a continuous stream of white flares and orders all tanks to switch on their headlights. The enemy tanks are illuminated as bright as day...

During the rounding-up and disarming of enemy troops, a British officer managed to set fire to some of his tanks, before he was detected and taken prisoner. This victory by I.*Abteilung* brought the following success: Capture of what remained of the 4th Armoured Brigade, the brigade leader, 17 officers and 150 NCOs and troopers, one command tank, 35 tanks and several armoured cars, and a large amount of supplies. Also important operational documents were captured...

A further report from the same unit dated 25 November 1941:

On 25 November 1941, the regiment advanced to Sidi Omar in presence of both the commander-in-chief of the *Panzergruppe* and the supreme commander of the *Deutsches Afrikakorps*. At 10km west of Sidi Omar heavy artillery fire and strafing aircraft affected the regiment... At around 14.00hrs, 1.*Abteilung*, acting as the spearhead of the division, is attacked by 20 Matilda IIs. At the same time the regimental commander pushes 2.*Abteilung* forward to the left of 1.*Abteilung*. The enemy now faces a broad battlefront at close

Above:
In 1941, the 7.5cm *Grenate* 39 HL/A hollow-charge shell became available, and this allowed the PzKpfw IV to fight heavily armoured tanks such as the Matilda II with some success. This PzKpfw IV Ausf D has a stowage bin fitted to the rear of the turret, distinctive item on the tanks of PzRgt 5. (Hoppe)

Above:
Frequently, *Panzerpioniere* were forced to improvise due the shortage of specialized equipment. Here they have fabricated a simple carriage using an axle with two wheels for moving bridging sections. These would be towed into position by PzKpfw II to allow passage over an obstacle such as an anti-tank ditch. (Anderson)

range (600 to 800m) and attacks with little commitment. Reinforced by 8.8cm Flak, a fierce combat ensued and the majority of the enemy tanks were destroyed, only three tanks retreated… 17 Matilda IIs and numerous support vehicles were left burning on the battlefield. Our own losses are low, only one prime mover of the 3.FlaKRgt 33 was destroyed by a direct hit…

By the end of 1941, Rommel had achieved a stunning success on the battlefield and had proved himself to be an ingenious operational commander, a brilliant tactician able to predict the movements of his enemy. Against all odds, Rommel and his *Afrikakorps* always managed to turn a defeat into a victory. He was a master of mechanized warfare and the *Panzerwaffe* allowed him to achieve his success.

However, in some areas Rommel failed: the Hero of German and British propaganda, the *Wüstenfuchs* (Desert Fox) was not a strategist, and although officially subordinated to Graziani, he stubbornly ignored orders and the command chain, avoiding any cooperation and dismissing all warning signals.

The German supply chain relied on the sea route from Naples to the ports of Tripoli and Benghazi. Since the Enigma code had been broken, the supply routes and shipment dates became known to the British, and the RAF positioned on Malta proved to be a deadly danger to German shipping. The following table shows the tonnage lost in 1941.

Month	Percentage of tonnage lost
June 1941	4.4
July 1941	19.5
August 1941	13.5
September 1941	28
October 1941	20
November 1941	62
December 1941	18

The decision not to take Malta is understandable as Rommel's unauthorized rapid advance to the border Egypt tied up valuable forces. Furthermore, the planned invasion of Soviet Russia required the assembly of enormous resources. Another reason was the extremely costly invasion of Crete; a repetition of which was apparently not wanted.

Also the *Luftwaffe* units stationed on Sicily were overburdened. Their assigned tasks – protect German shipping, eliminate the RAF on Malta, attack Royal Navy ships protecting convoys and patrolling the North African coast and also to attack enemy ground forces – were unfeasible.

After Operation *Crusader*, Egypt and the Suez Canal were secured, and the siege of Tobruk lifted. The *Afrikakorps* had only a relatively small number of tanks in combat condition to secure their position and were subsequently pushed back to their original lines.

Below:
The *Panzerjäger-Abteilung* (PzJgAbt) 605, equipped with the 4.7cm PaK(t) auf PzKpfw I Ausf B self-propelled anti-tank AT gun, was sent to North Africa to reinforce tank destroyer companies. The 4.7cm PaK(t) was generally considered as being accurate and hard hitting, but the PzKpfw I chassis was not strong enough to carry the weight of gun and armour and proved to be unreliable. PzJgAbt 605 arrived with 27 of these vehicles. (Hoppe)

CHAPTER 11

UNTERNEHMEN MARITA

The unwanted campaign

On 13 April 1939, Italian forces began the occupation of Albania and a few weeks later, on 22 May 1939, Germany and Italy signed a 'Pact of Steel', a political and military alliance. The government of Greece felt threatened by the presence of Italian forces on its border and improved their defences. On 28 October 1940, Italian forces attacked, but after several weeks of heavy fighting the Greek army had pushed the Italians back to Korçë (Koritza) in Albania by 22 November 1940.

The defeat caused great consternation in the German *Reich*. Hitler had already made his decision to invade and confirmed this in his directive No. 20 dated 13 December 1940:

F.H.Qu., den 13.12.40

Der Oberste Befehlshaber der Wehrmacht
OKW/WFSt/Abt. L (I) Nr. 33406/40 g.K.Chefs.

Geheime-Kommandosache
Chef Sache
Nur durch Offizier

Weisung Nr. 20
Unternehmen *Marita*

Left:
PzKpfw II tanks of
2.*Panzerdivision* cross a
bridge which has been
partially destroyed by
retreating enemy forces.
For *Unternehmen Marita*
2.PzDiv was reassigned to
the XVIII Mountain Division
of 12.Army. (Getty)

Above:
A PzKpfw II from the *leichte Zug* (light platoon) attached to the regimental staff PzRgt 3 of 2.PzDiv. By this time, a commander´s cupola with vision slots (to improve observation of the battlefield) had been fitted to a large number of PzKpfw II tanks. Protection for the hull was improved by welding a box-like armoured-steel section over the rounded bow. Also additional was bolted on the turret and the front of the superstructure. (NARA)

1. The end of the fighting in Albania is not in sight. Facing the dangerous situation in Albania, it is most important to avoid the creation of British airfields to menace the Romanian oil fields.
2. It is my intention to:
   a. gradually build-up our forces in southern Romania
   b. deploy this group of forces at the beginning of favourable weather conditions (possibly in March) to take control of the north Aegean coast and, if necessary, of the entire Greek mainland [*Unternehmen Marita*]…'

At the end of the 1930s, the Kingdom of Yugoslavia had established friendly contact with the German *Reich* and entry to the Tripartite Pact (Axis) was discussed. However, when Hitler issued an ultimatum for Yugoslavia to join the Axis on 10 March 1941, anti-German demonstrations were organized. These culminated in a *coup d'etat* organized by General Simovitch on 27 March 1941.

At this moment Hitler decided to expand his invasion plans and seize Yugoslavia. In a conference with leading military and political personal, he described the situation in the Balkans:

The *Führer* described the situation in Yugoslavia in the aftermath of the military coup. He determined that Yugoslavia is a weak factor concerning the coming *Marita* action and even more for the coming *Unternehmen Barbarossa*... The *Führer* is determined to make all preparations to crush Yugoslavia without waiting for possible declarations of loyalty. The attack will take place upon preparations being concluded... In a political sense, it is important to deliver this strike against Yugoslavia with unrelenting might. This will deter Turkey... the coming offensive against Greece will be favourably influenced.

In this context the starting date for *Barbarossa* has to be postponed by four weeks...

In his directive No.25 Hitler ordered:

F.H.Qu., den 27.3.41

Der Führer und Oberste Befehlshaber der Wehrmacht
OKW/WFSt/Abt. L (I Op) Nr. 44379/41 g. K. Chefs.

Geheime-Kommandosache
Chef Sache
Nur durch Offizier

Weisung Nr. 25

1. The military coup in Yugoslavia had changed the political situation in the Balkans. Yugoslavia must be considered as an enemy, and subsequently crushed.
2. My intention is a concerted operation... to establish a base for the continuation of the Italian-German offensive against Greece. The opening of the river Danube for traffic and the occupation of the copper ore mines at Bor are very important to our defence industry. As to the regaining of the Banat region and Macedonia, both Hungary and Bulgaria may be convinced to participate in these operations...

By the beginning of April 1941, the Germans had deployed two armies bordering the Balkans.

The 2.Army (including 8. and 14.PzDiv) were positioned in Austria, Hungary and Romania, ready to invade Yugoslavia and take control of Belgrade and the rest of the country. If necessary, it could be supported by 12.Army, which was positioned in Bulgaria ready to advance through Albania.

The OKW anticipated much higher resistance from British and Greek forces, so the tank detachment was significantly increased (2, 5, 9 and 11.PzDiv). As a reserve, the 4.PzDiv was alerted, but it was anticipated that it would not be required until 22 April.

Above:
Led by a PzKpfw I Ausf B *Ladunsleger* I (Explosive-charge layer), tanks of the *Panzerpionierkompanie* (PzPiKp) of 2.PzDiv advance to new positions in the Balkans. The commitment of a *Ladungsleger* could be decisive, as many after-action reports suggest. However, it was a dangerous operation, as the vehicle had to be reversed to the target making it very vulnerable to most anti-tank weapons of the day. (NARA)

Right:
The Metaxas Line, on the border between Albania and Greece, was formed from concrete obstructions, steel and barbed-wire obstacles also numerous anti-tank ditches. (Vargis)

The four *Panzerdivisionen* had a total of 18 PzKpfw I, 260 PzKpfw II, 125 PzKpfw 38(t), 109 PzKpfw III (3.7cm), 131 PzKpfw III (5cm), 122 PzKpfw IV and 43 PzBefWg (command tanks) available. Most of the tank companies were still not fully provided with PzKPfw III or IV according to KStN 1175 (see Chapter 9). The proportion of 5cm armed PzKpfw III was increased to more than 50 per cent.

Note: 54 *Sturmgeschütze* (7.5cm KwK L/24) were available during this campaign. These assault guns were under the control of the artillery, intended as direct support for infantry units.

The attack

On Sunday, 6 April 1941, German forces simultaneously invaded Yugoslavian and Greek territory.

On the same day, the *Luftwaffe* reported a sweeping success against the Yugoslav air force, and Belgrade was bombed three times. The new Yugoslav regime was not able to establish orderly resistance. While 14.PzDiv met only weak enemy forces, 8.PzDiv was involved in heavy fighting at Slatina. On 12 April, Belgrade was taken without a fight and the country capitulated on 17 April 1941.

Greece was attacked in three divergent thrusts. An eastern group attacked Thrace in a limited advance. The centre group attacked the Metaxas Line at Fort Roupel and the north-west group advanced through Yugoslavia. Skopje was taken on 6 April, with the Monastir gap being the next objective. Here

Above:
A PzKpfw III Ausf F, still mounting the 3.7cm gun, carries the official (a divided circle) and the unofficial (charging ghost) emblems of 11.*Panzerdivision*. The tanks of PzRgt 15 had two-digit turret numbers only, denoting the vehicle and the platoon number. The company identifier marking was painted on a rhomboid-shaped plate. (Hoppe)

Above:
A column of PzKpfw IIIs on a mountain road near the Albanian border which has been widened by *Panzerpionier* troops using explosive charges. Many were disabled due to loose stones entering the running gear causing serious damage. According to action reports from workshop units, the most serious were the road wheels and leaf springs on the PzKpfw II which failed in large numbers, almost equalled by the road wheels on the PzKpfw III. (Anderson)

the group separated, one attacked the Hellenic Army in Albania, the other rushed south.

All three forces were to converge on Thessaloniki. After the capture of the city, three panzer and two mountain divisions were to be made available for the follow-up thrusts toward Athens and the Peloponnese.

The mountainous border region which separated Bulgaria from Greece caused many problems. After fierce defensive fighting by Greek troops the Metaxas Line, at Fort Roupel, was finally broken by *Gebirgsjäger* (Alpine troops).

On 13 April 1941, *Generaloberst* Halder noted in his war diary:

Thus far reports of own losses are gratifying (400 casualties, 1,900 wounded, and expenditure of ammunition is low.

On 23 April 1941, King George and the Greek government abandoned Athens and fled to Crete leaving the country to the German occupiers. Two days earlier, British forces had begun their evacuation to the island of Crete (captured by German forces on 1 June 1941), which would allow them to control the Aegean Sea and to launch air raids far into Romania.

2. *Panzerdivsion* in Greece

PzRgt3 of 2.PzDiv attacked from their holding positions in Bulgaria and advanced into Macedonia. From an after action report:

> ... a deep anti-tank ditch and concrete obstructions halt the advance. The enemy fires with machine guns and anti-tank guns. The lead platoon of *Leutnant* Brunenbusch opens fire on the enemy, who has taken positions on the opposing slope in a dense thicket. The remaining platoons sheltering in the trench are trying to find a crossing, but cannot proceed. One tank after another hits a mine and is disabled. Due to the dense thicket, use of these weapons is impossible. The 7.5cm platoon, intended to support the lead platoon in the centre, also hits mines and stops. Finally our pioneers, covered by fire from the remaining tanks, Flak and machine guns, create a mine-free track. The *Panzereierleger* (lit. 'egg-laying tank', a synonym for explosive-charge dropping vehicles) succeed in blowing up the anti-tank obstructions and our motorized infantry defeats the enemy positions on both sides of the track. Now the Panzers can advance... Soon we are stopped again. Shortly after, two Panzer IV of 1.*Kompanie* also the staff section along with the reconnaissance and pioneer sections cross a bridge, but it is quickly destroyed by enemy fire. Our infantry is slow in advancing; again the tanks were too fast. Despite our leading forces being weak, Strumica is taken. One tank "conquers" a gun emplacement. Single enemy positions in houses, from which the battalion commander is fired at, are silenced by some HE rounds...
>
> The advance cannot be carried on until the next day after the road through the pass is taken... The division advances unopposed over the winding mountain pass, crossing countless bridges but is hindered by many craters caused by explosive charges. Our pioneers work continuously. Later this day, 12 Serbian tanks are surprised and all are destroyed. On 8 April, the Greek border at Lake Dorian is crossed. After a speedy ride we reach the gates of Thessaloniki. The city is handed over the next day, and German tanks parade through the streets...
>
> On 15 April, the division reached Panteleimonos and encountered heavy resistance from British forces, which had established artillery positions on a ridge near the peak of the Mount Olympus. In close cooperation with motorized infantry and motor-cycle troops the entire *Abteilung* attacks. The first thrust against the ridge fails due to the difficult terrain. Overnight the tanks breakthrough the concrete anti-tank defences. The next day the *Panzerkompanie*, supported by pioneers on its right flank, manage to advance through heavy scrub and rocks, and finally take the ridge.
>
> The tanks manage to advance on a very narrow donkey path. Many tanks fail due to lost tracks or broken suspension caused by the many rocks.

Bridges were vital for the swift advance through the mountains of the Balkans as many had been destroyed by partisans or the retreating defenders. This forced the German forces to ford numerous streams, which caused numerous breakdowns and some losses. Here a PzKpfw IV, followed by two PzKpfw III, crosses a stream protected by steep banks. (Anderson)

Finally, the lead platoon is halted by mines and totally block the way. Two further tanks trying to find another way become stuck in a swamp; a third explodes after a striking a mine. Road wheels, track links and parts of the turret fly everywhere, the wreckage burns…

With its few remaining tanks, 1.Kp attempted to take the old fort on the ridge. The steep and narrow mountain roads with their numerous turns proved almost impossible to be negotiated by the heavy vehicles. German pioneers had to widen them by blasting away the rocks. During the continuing pursuit of British forces, the way down was even more difficult. The unit had numerous failures due to constant damage to the suspension and running gear. The number of PzKpfw II, which were said to be better suited due to its size, left running was very few. Furthermore, their leaf-spring suspension proved to be very delicate. When the coast was finally reached, the railway line could be used to continue the advance.

The report continues:

… The stone walls of the Tempi ravine are steep… The only road, which could get us further, runs on the other side of the River Pineios: But how to cross the torrent? Finally, *Leutnants* Brunenbusch and Schmitthenner find a crossing after swimming through the river. A Panzer II dashes down the embankment into the water. Like a walrus the tank powers through the water, leaving only

Below:
A PzKpfw III has stalled on reaching the riverbank, due to the engine compartment becoming flooded with water. A situation like this was highly dangerous, especially if enemy forces were operating in the vicinity. (Zöllner)

the turret visible. The driver carries on unperturbed, despite sitting in water and his sight obscured by a bow wave… Now a further five tanks, one after the other, roll into the water. Two tanks sink but the crews manage to escape…

The fighting showed that a concentrated assault by combined forces – tanks, motorized and mountain infantry and also reconnaissance units – can be successful even in a mountainous area. PzRgt 3 finally reached open ground and advanced toward Larissa.

The commander of I./PzRgt 3 decided to move a PzKpfw IV from his heavy company to reinforce the light companies. This decision was both understandable and target oriented. The long-range 7.5cm HE rounds proved to be a significant help when fighting a dug-in enemy or one concealed in heavy scrub.

The after action report also mentions the deployment of heavy pioneer equipment. *Ladungsleger*, tanks mounted with explosive-charge dropping devices, were used to great effect to destroy concrete anti-tank obstacles.

Despite many technical breakdowns caused by the rocky terrain, there were still enough operational tanks available to continue the pursuit of the retreating enemy.

9.*Panzerdivsion*

The 9.PzDiv with PzRgt 33 was held for the attack further north, some 50km southwest of Sofia, Bulgaria. The 1.Kp/PzRgt 33 submitted an after-action report:

Above:
A column of PzKpfw III has been halted in a flooded area. Pioneers have established a safe path through the barrier and marked it with white tape tied to posts. The leading PzKpfw III carries two spare wheels and a section of track on the front. (NARA)

Above:
The 3.7cm KwK main gun and mantlet on a PzKpfw III, Ausf E or F, in service with 11.*Panzerdivision*; the charging ghost emblem is clearly visible. Again the combination of the rhomboid symbol and numbering is used, this time a one digit number indicating that it is from the staff section of a company. (Hoppe)

On 5 April 1941, the company is subordinated to *Vorausabteilung* (advance detachment) B and moves into assembly area west of Kyustendil. The commander of the advance detachment orders the following battle structure:
Two Panzer II: as reconnaissance vehicles (led by *Leutnant* Nusch)
Two Platoons: as an armoured spearhead
Pioneers and motorized riflemen on SdKfz251
Rest of company with three minutes delay
Four Panzer IV (led by *Leutnant* Becker)
Furthermore the *Vorausabteilung* includes:
One *Panzerpionier-Kompanie*
One motorized rifle company on SdKfz251
One sIG company (15cm sIG 33)
One battery 8.8cm Flak
One light howitzer battery
One platoon 2cm Flak

... On 6 April, the *Vorausabteilung* advances and takes a bridge at Kriva Palanka, which is set on fire. In attempting to cross the river an anti-tank obstacle has to be negotiated. In attempting this, a Panzer III breaks down. After removing the obstacle, the tanks proceed and join up with the four Panzer IIs which have managed to cross the burning bridge. Some 4km east of Kriva Palanka we open fire on the dug-in enemy. These forces were already pinned-down by the armoured reconnaissance section which was reinforced by the heavy weapons... *Leutnant* Grimm takes the lead with his Panzer III platoon and the four Panzer IIs... On the 10km dead-straight road the tanks advance at high speed... During this fast advance two Panzer III (5cm) fall out for mechanical reasons... Now the armoured spearhead approaches the Stracin Pass, which has two ridges allowing good observation. No enemy forces can be detected. The countless hairpin bends are negotiated by our tanks without problems. At the last bend, the leading Panzer IIs are suddenly hit by anti-tank guns. The following Panzer II and III open fire at the muzzle flashes of the AT guns. At the same time enemy artillery opens fire from positions on the ridge. Within half a minute, the four Panzer IIs are destroyed. The Panzer III is hit three times, which causes only some splinters in the interior, slightly wounding *Leutnant* Grimm ... Under assistance of *Gruppe* 'Gorn' and 'Schnalz', a second attack is launched which is successful. Several hundred prisoners are taken, four anti-tank guns and six artillery guns are captured...

... On 8 April, the company again is once again at the head with six vehicles, after motorcycle troops have taken the heights at Skopje:

Feldwebel Rüdiger	(Pz III)
Leutnant Grimm	(Pz IV)
Oberleutnant Grüner	(Pz III)
Company Commander	(Pz III)
Unteroffizer Pistrol	(Pz III)
Feldwebel Weber	(Pz II)

The first 10km over open terrain are quickly crossed despite enemy air raids... Later, the armoured spearhead succeeds in stopping the enemy preparing to blow up an important bridge at Kazanlak... After removing the many temporary tank obstacles made from rocks and wood, the lead vehicles reach Kazanlak. After rounding a bent, the three leading tanks receive many hits from 4.7cm anti-tank fire. Firing smoke very effectively, the Panzer IV blinds the enemy anti-tank gun positions. The other tanks open fire, and in a fierce firefight all four guns are silenced. During further combat several hundred prisoners are taken, among them 14 officers and one regimental commander. The captured unit was a retreating British Hussar regiment...

Above:
A PzBefWg of PzRgt 31, 5.PzDiv, at full speed. Both rod aerials mounted on the sides of the superstructure are folded down. The vehicle appears to have been fitted with the wider 40cm track; note the spacer visible on the drive sprocket. (Hoppe)

This report reveals the variety of support elements which were available within the 2.*Panzerdivision*. At best the company would have been provided with five PzKpfw II, 12 PzKpfw III (3.7 and 5cm) and four PzKpfw IV. Considering the assigned task as a lead column, the unit was further reinforced by infantry guns of the sIG Kp 703 (15cm howitzers mounted on the chassis of a PzKpfw I), 2cm Flak guns of the PzJgAbt, also light field artillery and 8.8cm Flak guns, provided by a *Luftwaffe* field unit.

The *Panzerwaffe* in the Balkans

The complete Balkans campaign was at no time what could be called 'a classic tank war'. Neither the Yugoslavian nor the Greek army had large tank detachments. Even the British had an insufficient number of tanks, having only 1st Tank Brigade of 2nd Armoured Division available and this was equipped for desert warfare rather than for the mountainous terrain of Greece. The commitment of tanks was reduced due to determined attacks against Greek troops in dug-in positions and the concrete and barbed-wire anti-tank defences of the Metaxas Line. As shown in the after action reports, rather than making large-scale attacks with complete tank battalions or even a regiment, single companies were sent into action, supported by specialized forces such as artillery or pioneers. However, the fast Panzer proved to be most valuable in pursuing the retreating forces.

German tank divisions suffered a manageable number of total losses. A total of ten PzKpfw I, 13 PzKpfw II, seven PzKpfw 38(t) also 21 PzKpfw III and eight PzKfw IV had to be written off due to enemy mines or anti-tank gun fire. Many of the failed tanks were temporarily out of action due to mechanical damage, which could be repaired. The damage caused by the very difficult terrain – worn-out brakes and steering gear – was indeed significant. By end of April, nearly all tanks of the involved *Panzerdivisionen* were in need of major maintenance.

The German intervention in the Balkans and in North Africa, had consequences for the course of war. In North Africa, precious combat troops and supplies were tied down. In Yugoslavia, a most brutal partisan army emerged and fought with a vengeance that led to many atrocities being committed by *Wehrmacht* units in retaliation.

Below:
German soldiers examine a PzKpfw III Ausf E or F which had possibly struck a mine to see if anything is salvageable. A total of 21 PzKpfw III had to be written off due to mines or ant-tank fire. (Anderson)

CHAPTER 12

BARBAROSSA —
OFFENSIVE IN THE EAST

Late in 1940, Adolf Hitler made his decision to invade Soviet Russia in contravention to the Non-Aggression Pact signed by Molotov and von Ribbentrop on 23 August 1939. The pact was partly a trade agreement from which Germany was to receive raw materials in exchange for technical equipment.

In the following months, the Soviet Union occupied the Baltic States and Bessarabia (Moldova). On 30 November 1939, Soviet forces attacked Finland, and after 14 weeks of bitter fighting the country surrendered on 13 March 1940, but maintained its independence.

In 1940, the German ministry of economics informed Hitler that despite deliveries from Russia, the amount of raw material supplied would be insufficient to support the coming war against Britain and her allies. Furthermore, the German *Reich* was reluctant to supply modern technical equipment and lacked the financial resources to make any payments.

An invasion and subsequent control of this vast nation would solve many problems: Germany would become blockade-proof. In December 1940, Hitler had finally decided to launch the offensive with the code name *Unternehmen Barbarossa*. On 30 March 1941, during a briefing of 200 officers, Hitler stated that the coming conflict was to be an ideological war of race annihilation which was to be pursued without any consideration to the law of nations. The catastrophe was to begin…

Left:
Elements of an unknown PzRgt cross a stream somewhere on the newly established *Ostfront* (East Front). The lead vehicle is a PzKpfw IV Ausf E, and is fitted with the narrow 38cm tracks, and has 30mm add-on armour bolted in front of the driver's position only. (Anderson)

Above:
The recovery of vehicles from the battlefront was very important. Here a damaged tank is being carried on a flat-bed (SdAnh 116) trailer, towed by a Famo-built s ZgKw 18t (SdKfz 9). The PzKpfw IV Ausf E has add-on armour bolted in front of the wireless/machine-gun operator's position but not in front of the driver; perhaps this was due to a shortage of material. (Münch)

On 31 January 1941, the *Oberkommando des Heeres* (OKH) announced:

Deployment instructions for *Fall Barbarossa*

Mission:
In case Russia is changing her previous position we will have, as a precaution, to make all provisions to defeat Soviet Russia before entering the war against Britain.

The operations have to be carried out in a way that the main part of their army, which is located in the western parts of Russia, will be annihilated by fast advancing *Panzerkeile* (tank wedges). The retreat of any remaining combat-ready elements into the vastness of the Russian territory has to be stopped…

Heeresgruppe Süd has the task of pushing forward its strong left flank, with her fast-moving forces ahead, towards Kiev in order to destroy the Russians in Galicia [Eastern Europe] and in western Ukraine to the west of the river Dnieper. The transport centres at the Dnieper and south of Kiev have to be taken to ensure continuation of the operation.

Heeresgruppe Mitte will push forward with strong forces at its flanks in order to scatter the enemy forces in White Russia. After passing Minsk, both flanks will join to take the region of Smolensk. The preconditions have now been set for the deployment of strong tank forces to combine operations with *Heeresgruppe Nord* in order to annihilate all enemy forces fighting in the Baltic region and around Leningrad.

Heeresgruppe Nord has been tasked to destroy the enemy forces fighting in the Baltic region and to occupy the Baltic ports, also Leningrad and Kronstadt, thus depriving the Russian fleet of their bases…

Above:
German troops cross the border (*Grenze*) and into the Soviet Union. A PzKpfw IV Ausf E, carrying a large number of jerry cans, passes some German infantry resting at the roadside. The only tactical marking visible is the three-digit vehicle number painted in white. (Münch)

Following to the successful completion of this phase of operation, the next target to be taken was Moscow and the industrial areas to the south of the city. Finally, a line from Archangel to Astrakhan was to be occupied which would allow unimpeded access to raw materials from the Urals and oil from the wells in the Caucasus region.

The *Panzerwaffe* was again chosen to spearhead the invasion which required 17 tank divisions to be mobilized; each had a slightly different organizational structure. Some 50 per cent of the *Panzerdivisons* contained three *Abteilungen* made up of two light and one heavy company each. The remaining two *Abteilungen* were made up of three light and one heavy company each. The complete armoured strength on the German side was as follows:

Strength of Panzerwaffe, June 1941

PzKpfw I	152	PzKpfw II	743	PzKpfw III (3.7cm)	259	PzKpfw III (5cm)	707
PzKpfw IV	439	PzKpfw 35(t)	155	PzKpfw 38(t)	625	PzBefWg	186
Sturmgeschütz	272						

	Combat Companies	PzKpfw I	PzKpfw II	PzKpfw 35(t)	PzKpfw 38(t)	PzKpfw III (3.7 cm)	PzKpfw III (5 cm)	PzKpfw IV	PzBefls-Wg	Sturm-geschütz	Sum of all types
1.PzDiv	6		43				71	20	11		145
3.PzDiv	9		58			29	81	32	15		215
4.PzDiv	8		44			31	74	20	8		177
6.PzDiv	9		47	155				30	13		245
7.PzDiv	12		53		166			30	15		264
8.PzDiv	9		49		118			30	15		212
9.PzDiv	6	8	32			11	60	20	12		143
10.PzDiv	8		45				105	20	12		182
11.PzDiv	6		44			24	47	20	8		143
12.PzDiv	9	40	33		109			30	8		220
13.PzDiv	6		45			27	44	20	13		149
14.PzDiv	6		45			15	56	20	11		147
16.PzDiv	6		45			23	48	20	10		146
17.PzDiv	9	12	44				106	30	10		202
18.PzDiv	9	6	50			99	15	36	12		218
19.PzDiv	9	42	35		116			30	11		234
20.PzDiv	9	44	31		116			31	2		224
18 StuG units	40 batteries									272	272
Sum Total		152	743	155	625	259	707	439	186	272	3,538

Note: *Heerestruppen* not included

The conversion of the PzKpfw III production lines to the 5cm gun version had been completed. In June 1941, more of the 5cm armed tanks (707) were available than the 3.7cm armed version (259). This meant that most tank divisions had substantial numbers of the Germany's main combat tank available. The exceptions were the 6, 7, 8, 19 and 20.PzDiv which were equipped with Czech-built PzKpfw 35(t) and 38(t), and also some Pzkpfw IV in their medium companies.

Challenging a sleeping giant

The Red Army had a far greater number of various light tanks (*c*.6,000) at its command as, since the early 1930s, the Soviet Union had undergone massive if not reckless industrialization. In the course of this, considerable funds were invested for the modernization of the Red Army and as a consequence the Russian tank force became the largest in the world. Reliable detail of numbers is difficult to obtain, and those in the table were taken from a Russian standard reference and show, with reasonable accuracy, the situation at the beginning of the war.

The German military knew of the Soviet advantage in the number of armoured vehicles. Both the T-26 and BT tank were correctly recognized as

Russian tank strength for *Barbarossa*, June 1941							
T- 27 (Tankette) MG	T-26 45 mm	BT-5 45mm	T-35 76.2mm	T-28 76.2mm	T-34 76.2mm	KV-1 76.2mm	KV-2 152mm
3,110	9,686	7,502	61	503	1,244	424	213

the main Russian battle tanks, but the multi-turreted T-28 and T-35 tanks were considered only as heavy support tanks. All the types were widely known to the Germans who had observed them in the Victory Parades held on May Day in Moscow, or in Spain. Despite the superior numbers of tanks, the *Panzerwaffe* was certainly ready to face the challenge.

However, these German estimations would be far from those of reality.

Unknown opponents

The German intelligence section responsible for *Fremde Heere Ost* (Foreign Armies East) failed completely and proved to be totally unaware of actual developments in the Soviet Union. In complete secrecy, the Russians had designed and developed two new types of tank; each had significant similarities but differed in many characteristics.

Below:
The amphibious T-37 tank is a good example of the thousands of light tanks produced by the Soviets before World War II. This series of tanks was developed, and the T-40 was the last amphibious tank produced in the war. (Anderson)

Above:
The T-34 came as a shock to the German *Panzerwaffe*. Armed with a powerful 76.2mm gun and a hull fabricated from sloped-armour plates, the type was almost impervious to fire from German tanks then in service. (Getty)

T-34

This medium tank was designed to support the BT-5 and BT-7 fast cavalry tanks. Being designed in the mid-1930s, these were light tanks built from relatively thin armour and mounted a 45mm gun. Towards the end of the decade, it was decided to develop a successor with an expanded field of duty: this would require a revolutionary approach to tank design. The new design was to have all-round sloped armour (a feature not seen on any contemporary tanks) of some 45mm thickness which gave excellent protection. The carefully shaped turret was fabricated from welded steel or a steel casting.

A Christie-type suspension consisting of five large road wheels damped by vertical coil springs mounted inside the hull was retained, but the option to run the tank without tracks was recognized as being ineffective and was subsequently dropped. Plate-type tracks, much wider than those on the BT, were fitted to give a very low ground pressure. The complete suspension was designed for the Russian battlefield; the tracks links did

not have any gaps and the road wheels did not have any apertures, thus wet mud could not clog the suspension. The tank was powered by a 38,800cc Model V-2-34 liquid-cooled V12 diesel engine developing 500hp extraordinary at that time. The result was very mobile, well-armed and armoured tank.

The T-34 was armed with a 76.2mm F-34 long-barreled gun, designed to fire both powerful armour-piercing (AP) and high-explosive (HE) rounds, and had a ballistic performance far superior to all other nation´s tank guns.

The KV

This heavy tank was introduced as a successor to the slow running and lightly-armoured T-26 infantry tank, and also the existing T-28 and T-35 heavy tanks as their multi-turret design was recognized being as obsolete. The chassis of the T-26 was much simpler than that of the BT fast tank, but both types utilized the same turret and gun. In order to

Above:
The KV-2 was the heaviest tank in Soviet service at the beginning of *Unternehmen Barbarossa*. As with its forerunner, the KV-1, it also had heavy armour which made it almost invulnerable to fire from German tank guns. The Opel Olympia staff car gives scale to the enormous size of the KV-2. (Getty)

replace the T-26, Soviet designers went even further and produced a completely new design: the KV (after Kliment Voroshilov, Secretary of Defence until 1940).

By pre-war standards, it had a more or less conventionally shaped hull, but the armour was extraordinary thick and gave even better protection than the sloped armour on the T-34.

The suspension consisted of six road wheels and three return rollers. The KV due to its high combat weight was fitted with steel road wheels. The tank was powered by the Model V-2-34 diesel engine (as used for the T-34) and had, despite its heavy weight, very good performance.

The KV-1 also mounted the same 76.2mm F-34 gun. A further variant, the KV-2 which mounted a 152mm howitzer in a massive turret, was intended for direct fire support.

The technical data tables below reveal the dramatic discrepancies in design philosophy.

Special purpose tanks in service with the German army

During the invasion of France (and the invasion of Poland), the German side introduced a small number of specialized weapons. Apparently the combat value of the *Panzerwaffe* was, at least in some parts, regarded as being inadequate for combat against heavy tanks, such as the French-built B1.

Type Technical Data	T-26 (1933)	BT-7 (1937)	T-34 (1940)	KV-1 (1940)
Armament	45mm L/46 one MG	45mm L/46 one MG	76.2mm L/30.5 two MG	76.2mm L/30.5 three MG
Crew	Three	Three	Four	Five
Penetration at 100m	42mm	42mm	92mm	92mm
Penetration at 500m	35mm	35mm	66mm	66mm
Penetration at 1,000m	28mm	28mm	58mm	58mm
Radio	Only command vehicles	Only command vehicles	Only command vehicles	Only command vehicles
Armour, frontal	15mm	15mm	45mm	75mm
Weight	9.2t	13.8t	26.8t	47t
Engine power	90hp	500hp	500hp	600hp
Max speed	31kph	52kph (on tracks)	55kph	34kph
Power/weight ratio	9.8hp/t	36.2hp/t	18.7hp/t	12.8hp/t
Ground pressure	0.63kg/cm²	0.85kg/cm²	0.62kg/cm²	0.77kg/cm²
Cruising range, max	182km	500km	455km	220km

Above:
A group of Red Army infantry, protected by the turret, hitch a ride on a T-34. (Getty)

An obvious and widely accepted solution to meet such a requirement was to develop _sebstfahrlaffeten_ self-propelled (SP) guns. Based on available chassis, half or fully-tracked, effective weapons could be mounted with or without armour protection.

Germany had obtained a large number of anti-tank (AT) guns after occupying Czechoslovakia. The 4.7cm PaK(t) had a ballistic performance that was almost comparable to the 5cm KwK L/42 and a decision was made to mount 200 on PzKpfw I Ausf B chassis fitted with an open lightly-armoured superstructure. The _Panzerjäger_ I issued to _Heeres-Panzerjägerabteilungen_ (army troops) were to be used for focal point attacks.

In an emergency situation, such as to defend against a tank attack or to provide protection for the flanks of their own tank attack, German troops deployed the 10.5cm _leichte Feldhaubitze_ (lFh) 18, also the 10.5cm _schwere Kanone_ K 18 and even the 15cm _schwere Feldhaubitze_ (sFh) 18. Although successful on a number of occasions, such action often resulted in the loss of the gun. Rapid repositioning was vital after an action, but in general proved to be difficult, if not impossible, under enemy fire.

The high-muzzle velocity 8.8cm *Flugzeugabwehrkanone* (Flak), proved to be more than adequate at destroying enemy heavy tanks at long range. The armour-piercing (AP) round was, by 1941 standards, of very heavy calibre and was very effective. The high-explosive (HE) round, which fragmented, was normally used against enemy aircraft, but also proved to be very effective when used in support of ground forces. However, deployment of the 8.8cm Flak was dangerous due to the difficulty of manoeuvring the weapon. During *Barbarossa*, a large number of *Luftwaffe* heavy Flak units were dispatched to army units to provide more fire power.

A small number of 8.8cm Flak guns were modified in order to optimize the weapon for the ground combat role. Ten were modified; a magazine carrying ready-to-fire rounds was attached to the gun shield which was also strengthened. These guns were mounted on semi-armoured *schwere Zugkraftwagen* (sZgKw) 12t tractor (SdKfz 8), providing them with greater mobility. The few after action reports available emphasize that these weapons could be quickly brought into position, and before enemy artillery could retaliate, the self-propelled (SP) guns were on their way to

Below:
Panzerpionier-Bataillone (PzPiBtl) 39 was equipped with an unknown number of *Brückenleger* (bridge-laying) vehicles based on the PzKpfw IV hull. The *Brückenleger* IVc (BL IVc), was designed to lay an 18m Krupp-built bridge consisting of two *Bockbrücken* (trestle bridges) within 12 minutes. The fact that the PzKpfw IV hulls used for the *Brückenleger* were old impaired combat readiness. (Anderson)

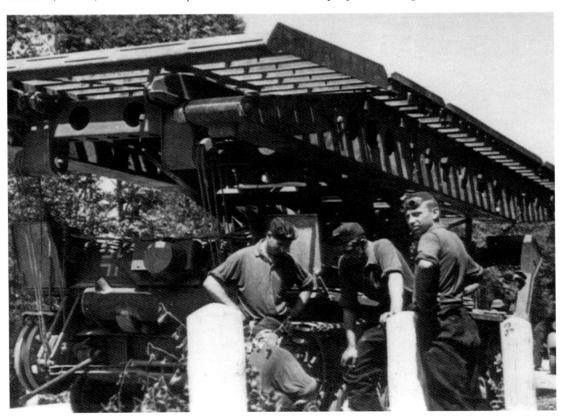

Above:
PzPiBtl 39, equipped with
BL IVc, has successfully
erected this bridge over
the Sczacara river on 25
June 1941, which allowed
the complete 3.PzDiv
and units of a motorized
division to cross. The
Bockbrücken would then
be taken up to be used
again at another location.
(Getty)

a new firing position. The 8.8cm Flak 18 Sfl auf 12t ZgKw were used, with some success, in the Polish and French campaigns. During Barbarossa, all were destroyed; the last vehicles were lost in early 1943.

A further 33 of these modified guns were mounted on trailers towed by armoured m ZgKw 8t (SdKfz 7), allowing fire to be opened without the trailer being unhitched. These guns were deployed in the independent PzJgAbt 525, 560 and 605, and were only used in action during the French campaign.

All these weapons were, despite their undoubted usefulness in combat, temporary measures. Possibly their successful deployment was due, in part, to the many shortcomings of the Soviet forces. Russian tanks had very poor optics which did not allow for clear observation of the battlefield, and the lack of radio equipment left a tank commander isolated. Furthermore, the tactical skills of many Soviet tank crews (due to poor training) was almost non-existent.

However, over the coming years many different versions of SP guns became the standard weapon of *Panzerjäger* (tank destroyer) units.

Left:
German tankers inspect
an abandoned Soviet KV-1
M1939 heavy tank which
has received more than
20 hits, but none stopped
this enormous tank.
(Anderson)

The turretless *Sturmgeschütz*, although designed as an infantry support vehicle, mounted the same 7.5cm KwK L/24 low-velocity gun as mounted on the PzKpfw IV. However, the *Sturmgeschütz* proved to be suited for combating Soviet tanks including the KV heavy tank. The difficult conditions on the eastern battlefield were no deterrent to the *Sturmartillerie* and as time would show, the *Ostfront* (East Front) was the ideal battleground for the *Sturmgeschütze*.

The attack

On 22 June 1941, *Fall Barbarossa* commenced as German troops crossed the western borders of the Soviet Union. The German assault was met by Soviet defenders who appeared shocked and helpless. It was days before all units of the Red Army were alerted and sent to the front, where they were met by scenes of pure chaos.

Leadership was poor; the officer's corps of the Red Army had been weakened by a number of purges ordered by Stalin. In the period before Barbarossa, three out of five marshalls, 13 of 15 army commanders, 57 of 85 corps commanders and 110 of 195 divisional commanders, together with thousands of lower-ranking officers were either executed or imprisoned in labour camps.

Furthermore, orders issued by the remnants of the command system were frequently countermanded by political commissars, who constantly intervened in the decision-making processes at the front line by demanding tactically useless and reckless frontal attacks; many of which resulted in an incredible number of losses.

The battle-proven German army utilized its strategic and tactical superiority, due to the speed of the advance many Red Army units were wiped out: entire Soviet armies were lost within days.

Commitment of *Tauchpanzer*

The western part of the Soviet Union is crossed by many great rivers and numerous smaller waterways, and also large areas are covered by swamps which provide a very effective natural barrier against an attacking force. In 1941, all existing bridges were strategic targets, however in this underdeveloped country bridges were a rarity, and many were destroyed by the retreating Red Army to slow the German advance.

All available *schwimmfähig* (amphibious) PzKpfw II and the submersible PzKpfw III(T) and PzKpfw IV(T) were brought to readiness for the invasion of the Soviet Union. On 14 May, *Panzergruppe* 2 commanded by Guderian, reported that the submersible tanks in four divisions, the 3, 4, 17 and 18. PzDiv, were ready for operations.

On 21 June, submersible tanks of the PzRgt 35 and PzRgt 18 were ordered to cross the river Bug. Unfortunately, all details of this operation have been lost.

In early July, the PzRgt 6 equipped with _Tauchpanzer_ was ordered to attack Soviet positions on the river Dnieper east of Bobruysk. From an after action report:

> By order of the commander of 3.PzDiv, Platoon Engelhardt (with three Panzer 3.7cm IIIa) was sent to the bridgehead at Sborovo, which was being menaced by advancing enemy forces. During the night, the platoon crossed under the Dnieper near Osserischtsche, and assisted in holding the bridgehead during the next day. During the fighting one tank was immobilized by hits, and then blown up when the bridgehead had to be abandoned. The next night, Leutnant Engelhardt drove submerged back to our side of the river. The return crossing of the Dnieper turned out to be difficult for the following reasons:
> 1. The water depth was approximately 3.5m
> 2. Firstly, a shallow place on the river bank had to be found
> 3. The bank had to be away from the swampy terrain to reach our bridgehead.
>
> The reconnaissance proved to be most difficult due to the heavy enemy fire. Furthermore, the _Abteilung_ realized that the same place could not be used for

Above:
Infantrymen climb on to a PzKpfw 35(t) and two PzKpfw IV of 6.PzDiv for transport to the front line. 6.PzDiv was the last one to be equipped with the Czech-built PzKpfw 35(t). During the advance to Moscow most would be lost either due to mechanical failures or to enemy action. (Getty)

the return of the platoon, since the northern bank was too steep. There was the danger of having to blow up all tanks for a possible abandonment of the bridgehead. Furthermore there were technical problems. Due to the previous diving missions and enemy fire, the majority of the rubber seals had been lost. Those tanks committed in fire fights had their seals blown off, and these would have to be renewed before a new diving mission. It should be noted that one of the two returning tanks had a fist-sized hole from a hit by an anti-tank gun, which had to be closed by ramming-in wooden wedges to prevent water entering. After many attempts we succeeded in recovering one tank from the steep river bank by harnessing together three heavy tanks and a prime mover. The commander of the second tank found a sandbank downstream and after another 200m submerged drive it was also recovered.

In this one action the *Panzerwaffe* had proven that amphibious and submersible tanks could be useful in a specific combat situation. Unfortunately, no other detailed combat reports have survived.

Panzerschreck (tank shock)

The majority of Russian tanks met in the first days of *Barbarossa* were either the T-26 infantry tank, or the BT-5/BT-7 light cavalry tank, both of which were of little value in combat.

Shortly after the beginning of the invasion, the *Panzerwaffe* was confronted by Red Army forces equipped with the new T-34 and KV-1 tanks, which were

Below:
A PzKpfw IV(T) of PzRgt 18: These specialized tanks required a great deal of preparation before being used for a submerged operation. However, the vehicles, even without full-waterproofing, proved to be a valuable asset for fording deeper rivers and streams. The unit emblem, a skull over water, is painted on the side of the turret. (Anderson)

committed in continuously increasing numbers. Although Red Army tanks were superior in performance they were still manned by insufficiently trained crews and fell victim to better German combat tactics. However, here was a warning of what was to come.

When facing these latest heavily-armoured types, German tank guns, and also towed AT guns in tank destroyer units, proved to be almost ineffective. The *Panzermann* (tanker) in his Panzer III had to realize that the given penetration data for his gun were of statistical value only. No German standard weapon was able to penetrate either the 75mm armour on the heavy KV, or the sloped 45mm armour on the T-34. The tungsten core *Sondermunition* (which was in scarce supply) designed for the 5cm KwK L/42 could penetrate the armour of the T-34 and the KV – but only if it hit at an angle of approximately 90°. Also any round hitting at an angle of around 30° would possibly ricochet off, making it virtually impossible to defeat the sloped armour on the T-34.

The smaller-calibre 3.7cm guns had absolutely no realistic chance of penetrating the armour on a Soviet tank, even if the round hit at what was considered to be a good angle.

Above:
A further PzKpfw IV(T), fitted with the water proof rubber cover over the gun mantlet, and also the hull machine gun. The *Fliegerbeschussgerät* 41, an anti-aircraft mounting for the MG 34. A large swastika flag has been draped over the top of the turret for air recognition. (Anderson)

Right:
Elements of a
Panzerdivision advance
towards a village, where
some houses have already
been set on fire by high-
explosive (HE) rounds.
The Pzkpfw IV Ausf D has
a number of modifications,
including a non-standard
stowage box mounted
on the rear of the turret,
and also brackets to carry
extra jerry cans and spare
road wheels. (Anderson)

The short-barreled 7.5cm KwK L/24 had a low muzzle velocity and had been designed to fire HE or smoke rounds, and thus had only weak armour-penetration capability; it also lacked accuracy. In late 1941, the armour-piercing (HEAT) hollow-charge round (7.5cm Gr38 HL/A) became available. This round could penetrate 70mm thick armour at any realistic range, and also it was less prone to ricochet off sloped armour.

It is obvious that these new Soviet tanks were unexpectedly strong adversaries for the *Panzerwaffe*. The T-34 (often referred to as 26t Panzer) could be stopped by hits, from close range, on the running gear or other weak spots from German tank guns. As the battle progressed, it became clear that determined action by a close-combat team could defeat a single tank. The lack of effective anti-tank weapons led ground forces to improvise: Bundles of hand grenades or explosives had to be used in many futile and dangerous attempts to immobilize an enemy tank.

On 9 July 1941, 3.PzDiv submitted an after action report dealing with the experiences of defence against Soviet tank attacks:

Soviet assaults with tanks

During the previous two days, 12 assaults were launched, of which five were assisted by two to five tanks. All Russian tanks which reached the German lines were put out of action, two by anti-tank rifles, one by PaK, and four by tanks positioned near the village road… a useful tactical deployment. Any cooperation by Soviet infantry with their tanks was not observed…

Below:
A factory-new PzKpfw III Ausf J (5cm KwK L/42) along with other tanks being replenished with ammunition and fuel during the summer of 1941. This version now has 50mm frontal armour as standard, but the crew has still placed extra track links on the front for increased protection. (Anderson)

It was clear that Soviet tank crews still lacked leadership and experience training to launch concentrated attacks.

From a further report of PzRgt 6 of 3.PzDiv dated 10 August 1941:

On 19 August 1941 at 05.30am, strong Russian forces attacked Unetscha from the northwest and tried with six heavy tanks of the type T-34 to enter the city via the bridge. In the city several tanks of I. and II.*Abteilung* were waiting for their workshop company. *Leutnant* Büschen moved to the north-western boundary with his Panzer IIIs (101 and 731) to defend against the enemy attack. The Panzer IV (412) had already taken position there and stopped a heavy Russian tank by a hit on the running gear. The crew abandoned the tank and escaped. Subsequently, a Panzer IV (412) was hit by another attacking Russian tank. Two further tanks were destroyed by Panzer III (101) some 70m before reaching the bridge... A further tank managed to enter the city despite heavy fire. *Leutnant* Störk in Panzer III (731) followed it. At the railway embankment the Russian tank was caught and set on fire by a demolition charge thrown into the engine compartment. After the rapid advance, Störk was ordered to meet the commanding general to be awarded...

Above:
A PzKpfw 38(t) of PzRgt 25, 7.PzDiv. This unit was the only one provided with an above average number (12) combat companies. The tank carries still a white air-recognition marking painted on the cover of the engine compartment, and the armament has been covered as protection against the ingress of summer dust. A number of 'Jerry' cans and boxes of machine-gun ammunition are packed on the vehicle; a hint to supply problems? (PeKo)

On 31 August 1941, PzRgt 6 submitted a further telling after-action report after their first encounter with the T-34:

> Assembled report on the impact of the regiment's weapons on Soviet T-34 tanks:
>
> The I.*Abteilung* destroyed three tanks with Christie-type suspension on 19 August. Clear penetrations were achieved using PzGr 40 only at favourable angles and at ranges below 400m, and only on weak points such as the gun mantlet or the hull sides. Binocular observation revealed that direct hits by PzGr 40 on the turret resulted in ricochets; even at ranges under 400m. Direct fire at the tracks resulted in clear penetrations, which however did not stop the tank due to the width the tracks. In one case, fire from 7.5cm rounds resulted in the crew abandoning their undamaged vehicle.

Below:
This PzKpfw III Ausf G proved to be too heavy (21.5t) for this wooden bridge. The crew survived this accident and the tank was recovered and returned to service. (Anderson)

Above:
Two PzKpfw IV of 7.PzDiv, move into position to cover both sides of a burning village. The tank to the left is an Ausf E, the one to the right is an Ausf D; both have been fitted with the new type of turret stowage box. The purpose of the hose fitted to '432' is unknown. (Anderson)

II. *Abteilung* did not achieve kills except for one T-34 which was destroyed near Unetscha by a *Leutnant* who placed an explosive charge in the engine compartment. Further T-34s in range of I.*Abteilung* were attacked by tank destroyers or artillery.

III.*Abteilung* with its 3.7cm guns was not involved in fighting against T-34s. Their gunfire would not have been effective…

On 22 October 1941, General Freiherr von Langermann, the commander of 4.PzDiv, submitted an after action report revealing an uncomfortable truth:

Subject: Fight against Russian heavy tanks

During its commitment, 4.PzDiv had several clashes with Russian heavy tanks. Initially these tanks were deployed individually only, and could be repelled by combined artillery fire. Under especially favourable conditions it was possible to destroy a single heavy tank by direct artillery hits. After the capture of Oryol, the Russian for the first time deployed his heavy and super-heavy tanks in a concentrated manner.

In several encounters very large tanks battles ensued, which could not be halted by our artillery.

For the first time in this campaign, the T-34 and KV proved their absolute superiority to our Panzer III and IV during this fighting. Deployed in a half-circle formation on most occasions, the Russian tanks opened fire with their 7.62cm guns from ranges of 1,000m, and penetrated our armour with great accuracy.

While our 5cm KwK could achieve penetrations, under most favourable conditions on weak points only and at very close range (50m), our tanks were hit at ranges of several hundred metres. Repeatedly our tank formations were literally split by these frontal attacks...

Apart from its superior gun, the T-34 is clearly superior in terms of its speed, agility and turret-rotating speed. The wide track enables it to cross streams, which cannot be negotiated by our tanks. The Russian tanks, due to having a lower ground pressure, can cross the same bridges as our vehicles, despite being heavier.

Left:
A German dispatch rider passes a column of abandoned Red Army T-26 light tanks, which by 1941 were obsolete and were destroyed in incredible numbers or abandoned by their panic-stricken crews during the German assault. (Getty)

The extraordinary diesel engine deserves special mention. During our advance from Glukhov to Mtsensk no Russian tanks were found having failed due to mechnical reasons. At the same time some 20 tanks of PzRgt 35 failed mechanically. It must, however, be mentioned that the Russian tanks were brand new…

Our tanks have much better observation means in the commander's cupola…

The above mentioned facts underline my impression that the Russian is fully aware of his technical superiority. In future he will employ his tanks decisively…. This will have negative effects on our *Panzertruppe*. Enthusiasm and morale of or troops will diminish, since our crews know that they can be hit from long range, while being unable damage the enemy despite having *Sondermunition* [tungsten-core ammunition].

This report appears to be excessive, if not panic-stricken, in its content but does reflect the actual situation. All German tanks had become outclassed

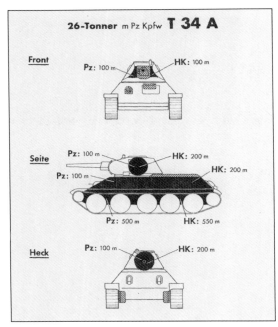

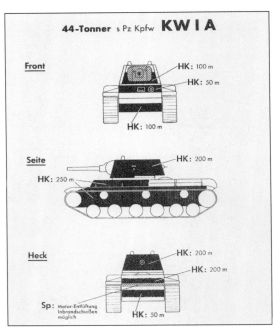

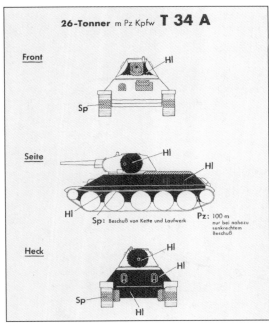

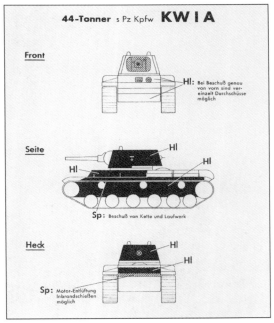

Above:

In late 1941, German tank gunners were issued with manuals detailing the best method of defeating an enemy tank. The charts at the top show the impact of the 5cm KwK L/42, the black areas show where armour-piercing or HK (tungsten core) rounds could penetrate. The bottom charts refers to the 7.5cm KwK L/24 firing high-explosive, HL (hollow charge) or armour-piercing rounds. (HDv 469/3b)

Above:
A Soviet-built KV-1 M1940 fitted with additional bolted-on armour plates. Apart from the 8.8cm Flak, no German gun was able to defeat this heavy tank. (Anderson)

Left:
The Germans were forced to make best use of all weapons available. Here an 8.8cm Flak 18 is being pushed forward by its towing tractor. As soon as a Soviet heavy tank was spotted, the gun crew would open fire despite being exposed to any enemy action. (Anderson)

Above:
Krupp designed and built two self-propelled heavy guns on the chassis of the PzKpfw IV Ausf A as *Schartenbrecher* (Bunker buster) tanks, which were designated 10.5cm K auf *Panzer-Selbstfahrlafette* IVa. The vehicles, occasionally referred to as 'Dicker Max' (Fat Max), were armed with a 10.5cm gun which had ballistic performance identical to the *schwere* 10cm *Kanone* 18. Both vehicles were delivered to PzJgAbt 521 and were used during the attack on the Soviet Union. (Anderson)

when the T-34 and the KV tanks appeared at the battlefront. General von Langermann continues:

… To combat the Russian tanks with 8.8cm Flak or 10cm Kanone alone is neither sufficient nor satisfactory as both guns are too clumsy to deal with the mobility of the fast enemy tanks. They will be easily observed when moving into position and subsequently will be open to enemy fire. In the tank battle between Oryol and Mtsensk alone, two 8.8cm Flak and one 10cm Kanone (indeed all guns available in this sector) were destroyed or overcome…

These experiences demand an improvement of our tank force within the shortest time, so that the German soldier of today will not meet enemy tanks like his father did in 1917-18…

For successful combat against the Russian heavy tank, we herewith submit the following proposals:

1. Creation of an offensive weapon against heavy tanks:
   a. Immediately copy and produce the T-34 and the usage of all T-34 and KV tanks captured intact… One company required per regiment.
   b. Installation of the Russian 7.62cm gun into the Panzer IV.

c. Introduction of a 10cm tank destroyer.

d. Development of a new type of multi-purpose ammunition using all available materials.

e. As an immediate measure…. Installation of the 5cm PaK in the Panzer III, even if the vehicle will be nose-heavy.

2. Creation of defensive weapons against heavy tanks

a. 10cm *Panzerjäger*, self-propelled or towed. Two guns per anti-tank company required.

b. Creation of improved ammunition

c. Dropping of 3.7cm PaK in favour of 5cm PaK respective usage of captured Russian 7.62cm PaK

d. Development of a more powerful mine to destroy the KV tank…

General von Langermann details some rather understandable wishes, most probably shared by the majority of all troops fighting on the Eastern Front. His observations clearly show the complete technical inferiority of German tanks in some very important areas.

Below:
A PzKpfw II from the light platoon of PzRgt 3, 2.PzDiv, has been fitted with add-on armour bolted to the font of the hull and turret. The vehicle has not been fitted with a cupola, proving that these parts were supplied only when available. (Anderson)

Right:
During the advance on Moscow; a PzKpfw II is being recovered from a stream by a PzKpfw III Ausf J, after breaking through the ice. Both tanks are camouflaged with white-wash paint which has obliterated any identifying markings. (Getty)

Above:
With onset of the winter, frost and snow changed everything. This white-wash painted PzKpfw IV, of an unidentified unit, travels across an 'arctic' landscape in the freezing cold of a Russian winter. (Anderson)

Summary

The German *Panzerwaffe* proved to be the decisive factor in the early campaigns of World War II.

At the end of 1941, German forces stood at the gates of Moscow. The months of October and November brought heavy rain, which turned terrain into thick mud almost paralyzing the movement of troops. While the tanks could just continue operations, all support forces and the supply columns became stuck. German forces became depleted as replacement troops and equipment did not reach their destinations. Despite this, several counterattacks ordered by Stalin were repulsed.

On 15 November, the ground froze in the falling temperatures and the roads and tracks became passable again. German tank forces moved again and attempted to close a pincer movement and surround Moscow. The deeply-staggered Russian lines of defence, stiff resistance and many heavy counterattacks culminating with the onset of winter and finally halted the final charge to isolate the city. General Guderian finally had to admitted:

We underestimated the enemy, the size of its country and the vagaries of the climate. All this is now reaping its revenge. Fortunately, I stopped [my forces] on 5 December, otherwise a catastrophe would have been unavoidable.

In early 1942, the *Heeresgruppe Mitte* submitted a study explaining the failure of *Unternehmen Taifun* (Operation Typhoon). If somewhat one-sided, and pathetic, it explains the situation adequately:

Review

On 15 November 1941, on the orders of the *Führer*, the *Heeresgruppe* again used its weakened forces for a final advance on Moscow. Its forces reached the gates of the city in a unheeded forward thrust. On 5 December 1941, the Russian winter showed all of its force with temperatures of minus 30°C. The winter hit exhausted and tired troops, positioned far away from their supply lines, and without winter clothing and equipment. Lacking weapons and equipment suited for these conditions, the *Heeresgruppe* had to go onto the defensive almost instantly.

Below:
The extreme freezing conditions experienced in December 1941 became a critical problem for men and vehicles. Grease, oil and other fluids would freeze or turn viscous and engines would not start. In a temperature of minus 45°C, member of a *Sturmgeschütz* crew, from StuG Abt 203, has lit a fire under the rear of the vehicle to heat the engine compartment. (Anderson)

The Russian, well aware of the harshness of their winter, had waited for this moment. On 7 December, the enemy launched a counterattack..., which was intended to destroy the German equipment, thus decisively weakening the army…

The *Führer* ordered: 'Hold your ground at any price…' For weeks the men of the *Heeresgruppe* fought for their lives. Despite thousands suffering from frostbite, significant casualties and considerable loss of equipment our troops resolutely defended every metre of ground. When the situation did not allow any other choice, the *Heeresgruppe* retreated due to lack of reinforcements and the difficult conditions to an established temporary *Winterstellung* (winter position).

Despite all measures taken by the leadership and self-sacrifices by the troops, especially the officer corps, in combat the *Heeresgruppe* could not avoid the Red Army cavalry corps breaking through our positions… opening a gap of 100km between 4.*Armee* and 2.*Panzerarmee* near Szuchinitschi…

In the following days, the 33.Russian army broke through the line between 4.*Armee* and 2.*Panzerarmee* to a width of 35km, the Russian 39. and 29.

Left:
The crews of these PzKpfw IVs Ausf F have solved the supply problems in their own unconventional manner. With no white-wash paint available to camouflage their tanks, they have soaked old newspapers with water and 'glued' them to the ice-cold metal surfaces. (Anderson)

Army heavily attacked the left flank of the 9.*Armee* near Rzhev…
… The German soldier never lost his superiority over the Soviet, who gained his success only by massed deployment of forces as a human steamroller…
… The struggle of the *Heeresgruppe* was complicated by the absolute lack of efficient railway transport services, which hampered the supply…

For the first time in World War II, the *Panzerwaffe* had reached its limits. The German war machine had been unable to produce enough replacement tanks and a regular supply of ammunition, even winter clothing was in short supply. Furthermore, the importance of an efficient line of supply which manifested itself in the vast open deserts of North Africa occurred again at the gates of Moscow.

The German tanks had also lost their advantage in technical superiority. The appearance of the T-34 and the KV tanks on the battlefield clearly showed the necessity for new more powerful guns with considerably better armour penetration. New tank types with significantly better mobility and armour protection were desperately needed. Would German industry be able to deliver?

INDEX

Acknowledgements

This book was written using information researched in several archives including, Bundesarchiv/ Militärarchiv in Freiburg, Germany, and the National Archives and Records Administration (NARA), Washington, USA. Also from a new internet-based project for the digitizing of German documents stored in the archives of the Russian Federation (search for germandocsinrussia). I have attempted to evaluate and understand the documents found there in context to their historical background. I have made minimal reference to post-war printed publication.

My everlasting thanks go to the late Tom Jentz, undisputedly the best expert on the history of German armoured vehicles. I recommend the reading of his outstanding *Panzer Tracts* to deepen knowledge of German armoured fighting vehicles (www.panzertracts.com).

Also my appreciation to the following individuals who have provided help, advice or photographs, in particular Peter Müller of Historyfacts, a true friend and advisor.

My thanks also to the following individuals who allowed me access to their collections of photographic material:

Florian von Aufsess, Joachim Baschin, Holger Erdmann, Daniele Guglielmi, Henry Hoppe, Peter Kocsis (PeKo Publishing), Michael Kümmel, Karlheinz Münch, John Prigent, Jürgen Wilhelm, Wolfgang Zimmermann

Further photos were obtained from NARA, also bpk images and Getty Images/Ullstein Bild.

And finally, my sincere thanks to my ever-patient editor, Jasper Spencer-Smith.

Bibliography

Chamberlain/Ellis, *Britische und Amerikanische Panzer*: J. F. Lehmanns Verlag
Duval, *Entwicklung und Lehren des Krieges in Spanien*: Neff Verlag
Guderian H., *Die Panzertruppen*: Mittler & Sohn
Guderian H., *Erinnerungen eines Soldaten*: Verlag Kurt Voswinkel
Halder, *Kriegstagebuch*, several volumes: Kohlhammer
Jentz, Thomas, *Panzertruppen* Vols.1 and 2: Podzun-Pallas
Panzer Tracts, several volumes: Panzertracts, Maryland, USA
Soljankin, *Tanks in the Patriotic War*, Vols. 1 and 2,: Eksprint, Moscow
Volckheim, *Die Deutschen Kampfwagen im Weltkriege*: Mittler & Sohn